How to Write Almost Anything Better—and Faster!

Also by Arthur Herzog

FICTION
Orca
The Swarm
I.Q. 83
Takeover (formerly L-S-I-T-T)
Earthsound
The Craving
Aries Rising
Glad to Be Here
Make Us Happy
Heat

NONFICTION
Seventeen Days: The Story of Katie Beers
The Woodchipper Murder
Vesco: From Wall Street to Castro's Cuba
McCarthy for President
The Church Trap
The War/Peace Establishment
The B.S. Factor

Thanks to Lucy Kommissar, Mike MacDonald, Kathy Erskine, and Marian Munson

How to Write Almost Anything Better—and Faster!

Arthur Herzog

Including an Afterword on Computers and Word Processing by

Daniel B. Diner, Ph.D.

A Hearthstone Book

Carlton Press Corp.   **New York, N.Y.**

For Leslie, with love

Contents

CONTENTS

Fear of Writing

Nearly everyone is scared of it, yet writing is something most of us must do. I will show you how to overcome the fear of writing and, in five easy steps, how to write better and faster.

The main reason for writing well is to express yourself clearly. Not just "creative" writing, but in the writing we have to accomplish in school, in our occupations, and in our social and family lives. Those who can express what they want to say with clarity, forcefulness, and grace have a tremendous advantage over the vast majority who cannot. A well written memo will bring better results. A well written term paper or business letter (a rarity, so be sure to edit yours), reflecting the mind behind it, deserves respect, a better grade, maybe even a promotion.

According to the Carnegie Study of Education, the ability to write is "the most important and the most neglected skill in school." Now you can add the office, factory, retail establishment, almost anywhere communication is necessary, to the list of places where one's writing skills are being neglected. Today, with the rapid growth of the so-called service sector, writing skills are becoming ever more vital, and those who can't write well could easily become occupationally obsolete.

One of the goals expressed by the 1990 National Governors' Association and the National Literary Act of 1991 is that, by the year 2000, every adult American will be literate and will possess the knowledge and skills necessary to compete in a global economy, as well as exercise the rights and responsibilities of citizenship.

You may be among the many who have the urge to write but believe you lack the basic skills, such as vocabulary and sentence structure. Though their value is incontestable, it's likely that your capabilities are greater than you think. Let's assume that you already possess the fundamentals or could easily grasp them, that you have the necessary taste and judgment, or can acquire them. Thus, defeatism may be only a symptom. Those who really want to write almost undoubtedly can. Desire is half the battle.

Even so, rather than encourage writers, people seem to discourage them from the start.

"Open book after book devoted to the writer's problems," notes Dorothea Brande in *Becoming a Writer*, "and you will find, well toward the front of the volume, some very gloomy paragraphs warning that you may be no writer at all." With such news, there's hardly any need to discourage you because you will have already discouraged yourself.

Writers—accomplished ones as well as would-be's—frequently doubt their abilities, and they will constantly ask themselves if writing retains an important function. So much information seems to be conveyed through looking and listening, particularly via television and computer networks, that writing is, as critic Hugh Kenner states, "an abnormal act" in today's electronic world. This isn't likely to spur you on. Even so, remind yourself that if the craft of writing is on the decline, there's all the more use for those who are accomplished.

The methods I'll describe for you herein are designed to increase confidence, and will help eliminate the writer's curse—fear—though never expect to lose it entirely. Fear of pain is part of our nervous system, and writing is pain. Good writing is, above all, convincing writing. Start by convincing yourself.

Many instructors stress mechanics like grammar, syntax, usage, punctuation, and spelling, as though attempting to avoid split infinitives, dangling participles and weak transitions will make you a writer overnight. This sort of advice borders on deceit since it raises expectations but neglects the nitty-gritty, the step-by-step decisions on how to plan, organize, and achieve your writing, and with what results. In other words, what may be most important is a system for putting words on paper, one designed to provide support and create a buffer against uncertainty.

I can't teach you to write—I doubt anyone can—but I can offer tips that will be useful along the way.

Step One: Psych Yourself Out

Before you write a word, take a hard look at your approach. Most of us don't just up and write, though a few lucky ones can. For almost any kind of writing, mental preparation is almost mandatory, and that's especially true for those who want a writing career.

Clutter is the enemy. Before writing, or even thinking about a specific project, clear your mental decks. Find a fulcrum in your mind (and emotions) from which to work freely and easily, without unnecessary complications, constraints, and excuses. You may have to rearrange your life, at home, at work, in school, in order to prepare the way. Examine, carefully, your outlook. Your attitude will determine and affect the work you achieve, or as importantly, fail to.

Organization must apply to your desk, even if you store information in a computer. Have files, neatly labeled. Don't let notes written on legal pads accumulate until you can't keep track of them. If you're working on more than one project at the same time (which in itself may be a good idea) don't let them commingle. The state of your desk may indicate the state of your mind. The neater the better.

"I won't be able to do it and anyway it won't come out right."

Self-defeatism, fear of failure, such banes are so commonplace that it's almost as if our society instills them into us as children, and even as adults, because we're more easily controlled. When negative voices sound in your head, don't muffle them. Let them out. Hear them for what they are—inner rats that gnaw. We are all subject to being their victims.

Writers don't set out to fail but sometimes, willy-nilly, that happens. It can't be helped. The possibility of failure must not discourage. Your teacher didn't like your essay...Try harder next time. The same with your boss's opinion about your report on how to market clotheslines.

There's little question that you can do it. How good it will be is something else. You won't make it better by feeling sorry for yourself.

FEELING SORRY FOR YOURSELF

That can be fatal. It erodes at creativity and stifles output. Feeling sorry for yourself is either the reason for, or the result of, anxiety. Either way, anxiety can lead not to steady habits of work but mindless hopping around, though some anxiety is natural and keeps you on your toes. (Financial anxiety may be useful too. It can make you work.)

It won't hurt to ask yourself whether you believe you're at the center of the universe. You'd be ashamed to admit it, knowing what a baby-thought it is, but if you so indulge yourself, then all the terrible things that happen to writers and writing would be aimed specifically at you. It was you they deliberately chose to criticize, reject, didn't pay enough attention to, or neglected.

Obviously, you're not so special but subject to the same circumstances as other people. What happens to you may have less to do with you and your efforts than you imagine. It's important to be objective.

Also, question yourself squarely on how much praise, recognition, money, and so forth you really require. It may well be, once you have settled accounts with the part of you that bought the party line on riches and success, that you don't need them or you have enough already, at least for now. Having rid your head of the call for gold and glory, you will be free to do better work, the real intention all along, and the key to success.

Try to remember that many writers have endured adversity without self-pity, well, without enough self-pity to stop them.

EXCUSES

Excuses to escape from writing can take a bewildering number of forms, some quite seductive. Considerable self-honesty may be needed to recognize them for what they are. Down deep they are all the same: Serpents like the one who operated in the garden of indolence called Eden. Eating the apple was followed by expulsion and hard work. (Have an apple for breakfast to remind yourself.)

I won't write today because: "I'm not in the mood." Ask the garbage man if he's in the mood for trash, or the actor, who plays the identical role every night, if he's in the mood. Mood is a disease of amateurs.

"I'm bored." So? Writing can be boring. It often is. What isn't?

"I have a hangover." A hangover is a circular excuse. You (or your conscience) may have figured you'd fail and, not wanting to fail, you got loaded, which is the next-morning reason not to write. (The same applies to drug use.)

"I have plenty of time." Another fear-of-failure manifestation. You wait long enough so that you don't have enough time to finish and be judged. You have an assignment: An article, a book review, a report. You procrastinate, you gamble (or pretend) that you have plenty of time. You can beat the clock, churn out the stuff at the last minute, you're sure. What you've done is to set up a built-in excuse for poor quality, again by circular reasoning, so you can tell yourself you lacked sufficient time.

"I'm too busy with my job," might say a would-be, after-hours writer. But how many writers had full time jobs and wrote anyway? T.S. Eliot. Wallace Stevens. William Carlos Williams. Louis Auchincloss. Dennis Smith. William Nolen. Joseph Wambaugh (when he was a cop). A job may even stimulate the unconscious, forcing it to concentrate and to work harder in the precious time available. The most productive factory is said to be the one with the fewest man-hours; perhaps that applies to writing as well.

If you find yourself saying: "I lack inspiration," write. Writers may experience bursts of creative activity but mostly they just slog along without the sensation of being inspired. Inspiration is normal for them; it's their stock-in-trade, it's second nature.

"I'm worried." Write.

"I'm stuck." Write.

"I have writer's block." Write.

"I just broke up with my lover." Write harder.

"I CAN'T BE ALONE"

A great many people believe they can't be alone.

Scratch the unconscious of the legions who always wanted to write, didn't or tried to, and gave up because they couldn't summon up the determination and you'll often discover not lack of ability but the fear of loneliness at the root.

They would rather occupy themselves in almost any other fashion just so there are people around to talk to, laugh with, touch. The lack of another human presence can't be tolerated because, for such folk, isolation creates insecurity or, rather, insecurity hates isolation. Constant other-people-needers demand the mothering a writer has to supply for himself or herself. You have to be your own parent, fulfilling your own needs.

That doesn't mean the writer is in solitary confinement. If you're having a people-fit, you can talk on the phone (tersely), chat with a neighbor or roommate, wave to passersby, duck into someone's office for a second. Unless you're of an hermetical nature, if you don't have a family it may be a good rule to arrange for company after your stint. Otherwise, for writers working alone, solitude is not the same as loneliness. It can not only be endured but appreciated.

Step Two: Sit Yourself Down

(Introducing the *Sitsfleysch* System)

Consider your habits of work. Now ask yourself if you were paying yourself a salary for writing, would you fire yourself for laziness, lack of concentration, low output or none? What's the answer? Come clean.

The productive putting of pen to paper, or hands to typewriter or word processor keys, has to be accompanied by another act, the placing of rump to chair long enough for something to happen—*sitsfleysch*, from the Yiddish, for "flesh that sits," pronounced zitsflesh. It signifies patience of an active kind. (The German *sitsfleisch* means much the same, but also conveys sedentariness.)

You may be told that writers are not in competition, which is true only in-so-far as a writer stays unpublished. Though the competition is faceless, writers clearly compete for sales, ads, reviews, for space in magazines and journals, to get on a publisher's list and to appear in bookstores and supermarket bookracks. (In the same way, competition exists in terms of writing ability for students, business people who vie for the opportunity to write the presentation, and so on.)

The determined writer has the better chance of succeeding. He who has *sitsfleysch* is ahead.

To develop *sitsfleysch* is an essential step to writing without wasting time and energy.

WRITERLY AMENITIES

Picture the writer in those thirty-year-old whiskey ads: Feet up on a cantilevered desk, office in pastel colors with an exposed brick wall and a fireplace, hanging ferns, a reclinable leather chair in the corner, a secretary ready to retype a draft ... if he or she ever writes again.

If you have notions about the grandeur of being a writer, forget them.

You don't need elaborate surroundings. In fact, not comfort but the lack of it may be superior. A cramped space may be an asset if it discourages sloth by reminding you of your purpose. Perhaps have a bed to lie on—daydreaming is productive—but your writer's chair should be less accommodating. A hard wood chair may reinforce *sitsfleysch* while cushioned ones (especially those that swivel or rock) may undermine it. A straight chair helps discipline and it's good for your back.

The same no-frills policy may apply to the view. To gaze at purple foothills, meandering streams, the quaint village square might be nice, but you aren't writing a postcard. A patch of sky will suffice, cloudless, if possible, but better to see outside the blank exterior of a warehouse or even to remove yourself from the window altogether and face a featureless wall. (Those who work in offices may also want to place their desks against a wall if permitted.) Remember the objective: To force your mind into a bright ball of creative intelligence, oblivious to all else.

DISTRACTIONS

Strict rules must be enforced or time will unravel like an old sweater.

If you can, find a place to work in by yourself. Into this inviolate cell no children, friends, colleagues, or other intruders are to be admitted during the hours (even minutes) you have established as yours. At home, use a lock if you must for emphasis, but no visitors, including spouse or mate. Let overnight guests depart in haste. You're at work.

Freeing yourself from distraction may be tough in a stereo-crammed college dorm or a busy office, but go to a library or wear earplugs and an eye shade if you need to make your point. Hang up a "Do Not Disturb" sign. Terrify them with rages, feigned or real. "Get the hell out of my space!"

You may wander from your lair once in a while for coffee or a soft drink but you may have to explain that simply because you don't seem to be working doesn't mean you're not in the midst of heavy cerebration. The point may be difficult for others to understand, but a creative fugue acquires a momentum of its own, and the reason you're walking around is to let an idea settle and harden.

Despite admonitions not to phone you during certain hours, friends do anyway. And if they don't, somebody else will. Toward telephone distraction several approaches can be tried, including not having a phone, but that seems extreme. Not answering is a possibility, but letting the phone ring will explode your concentration too. If messages are taken for you, you return the calls, you may miss the person, who calls you again, fails to find you, leaves another message, and you call back—a daisy chain that may enrich the phone company but not you. On the other hand, lengthy phone conversations during the writing period (except about your project) must be avoided absolutely.

A solution is the terse telephone style, and that requires courage because you may lose friends. Brevity will be mistaken for coldness and that is the risk. For some reason, perhaps the absence of a reassuring or disapproving face, the telephone seems to encourage garrulousness and repetition which you want no more than flies on the typewriter. Make your crisp "yes," "no," or "maybe" as amicable as possible and hope for the best.

Writers often have difficulty communicating the devastating effect of unscheduled interruptions. The hours you've spent organizing a thought may be blown when somebody strolls in to ask about dinner plans. You don't care! But you do agonize about the perfect word that you just lost and may not be able to retrieve out of the flux you found it in.

Arguments before or during the working day must also be forbidden, for you may be thrown off stride. Save the acrimony until later—it might pass. A good paragraph might even lead to good sex.

There are mates—according to Hemingway, Zelda Fitzgerald, wife of F. Scott, was one—who, from a childish need for attention, jealousy or spite, will deliberately try to prevent you from writing. The sabotage may be subtle, or denied, and you may have to ask yourself if you're not an accomplice because you'd really rather fight than write. If the problems continue despite your objections, you may have to contemplate joint therapy, a hideaway in the hills, or divorce. The threat may be sufficient.

Method

Procrastination being a constant hazard for writers,

let us proceed with the habits central to organizing work (the goal) and more reasons for non-accomplishment.

The first rule is: Leave nothing to whim and caprice—yours. Don't give chance a chance. Anticipate what would otherwise have been accidents and oversights—running out of typing paper in the middle of the woods a hundred miles from civilization is just the sort of goof to which writers are prone. (Of course, the writer's subconscious may have secretly wished to foul up.)

Regard your tools as virtually sacred. Suppose you (like me) are a scissor-and-transparent tape writer, constantly cutting and reassembling. You permit someone to borrow your scissors who forgets to return them and the day may be shot as you feverishly search for a second pair. Petty as it may sound, to guard your equipment zealously is to protect yourself against delays.

Never lend anyone a book you might want to use.

Before you pour forth, pay attention to how you will pour forth. Many writers are almost as ritualistic about their methods as voodoo priests.

"A working habit he has had from the beginning, Hemingway stands when he writes. He stands in a pair of his oversized loafers on the worn skin of a Lesser Kudu—the typewriter and the reading board chest-high opposite him.

"When Hemingway starts a project he always begins with a pencil, using the reading board to write on onion skin typewriter paper. He keeps a sheaf on the blank paper on a clipboard to the left of the typewriter, extracting the paper a sheet at a time from under a metal clip which reads 'These Must Be Paid.' He places the paper slantwise on the reading board, leans against the board with his left arm, steadying the paper with his hand, and fills the paper with handwriting. The page completed, he clips it face down on another clipboard which he places off the right of the typewriter.

"Hemingway shifts to the typewriter, lifting off the reading board, only when the writing is going fast or well or when the writing is, for him at least, simple: dialogue for instance."*

You might imagine Hemingway compulsively eating ice cream at the end of every paragraph, yet rituals like this may serve to give the writer support. Write standing on your head if you like, but once you've singled out a method stay with it until you've made a considered decision to change. Habits can equal discipline.

---

*Writers at Work, The Paris Review Interviews, Penguin Books, 1977–1981 (five volumes), 1977: pp. 218–219. These books provide an invaluable look at the subject, although they push a sort of writers' mystique that not only does little good but may be harmful.

Even the choice of writing implements may have significance. In the old days (we, in our almost desperate attempt to make the past contemporary, as if we don't believe in the present, sometimes forget how far back they are) writers like Hemingway and Faulkner pushed pencils, but lead is generally out of style, as is writing by hand. So many can't read their own penmanship because, knowing they'd type later on, they neglected it in school. Others went to schools where penmanship was no longer stressed.

Typewriters are faster, word processors supposedly faster still. Choose the modality that seems most amenable. The late John Gardner used the typewriter for essays and book reviews but wrote fiction in longhand. (He would seem to have regarded fiction as separate and more personal. A whim. Whims among writers are common but not necessarily helpful because they may be a function of ego.) If you use an electric typewriter, be sure you have a repairman who works fast—or a spare typewriter. I know a prize-winning author addicted to old Smith-Coronas who has a dozen of them.

The electric typewriter has many advantages— ease of fingering, no bothersome screen to watch, intimacy with the paper. But typewriters have been almost totally supplanted by computers, perhaps fatefully.

My hunch is the implement affects the style. Back when primitive instruments were used, sentences tended to be longer, as though a writer feared he'd run out of ink on his quill or the point of his lead pencil would break. *The technology of style* has never been explored so far as I know. Sentences created on typewriters seem to be shorter and on electric typewriters shorter still. Perhaps the impatient whir stirs writers on.

The word processor-computer adds yet another dimension, one that writers had better learn to live with. You would think, given the ability offered by the machines to move words around, that stylistic possibilities would be endless. But I suspect writing on the computer is often stilted.

That may be the result of the very luxuries computers offer. Spell and grammar check, memory bank, total record of earlier versions....Well, says the writer, I can always re-do it. He or she, of course, delays and soon—too soon—the version on the screen becomes the final.

So the problem of adequate rewriting (when is enough?) remains with the computer, only it's likely to be worse because the screen has a certain fixed quality, like letters graven in stone. Don't be fooled. Your computer product will need as much work as that composed with a typewriter, a pen, or a lead pencil. Maybe more!

HOURS

If I seem to stress machine-like efficiency, it's not out of disdain for the carefree existence. I do so because so many who fancy themselves writers, and even boast of it, lured by what they falsely assume to be glamorous, make themselves ridiculous through bad habits like long hours at bars. Writing, said Yeats, is a "sedentary, solitary trade," and has to be embraced as one. A grand master like E.M. Forster wrote only when he felt like it, but about Forster was something of the elegant English amateur who looked down, or pretended he did, on professionalism. You must not.

As in other trades, designated hours must be observed. Though the writer may have the happy luxury of selecting his own, the selected time should be followed with the strictness of a visit to the parole officer. No matter if nothing happens for a while. Walk around your lair, do pushups, curse, stare out the window, but stick to your hours.

Habit is everything: Set up a *sitsfleysch* system and don't deviate. For professional writers, nine to one and three to five means nine to one, three to five, a head cold notwithstanding. Writers with family responsibilities might have to resign themselves to starting early, before others rise. Some may prefer nights but late hours should be avoided—with them comes the built-in, excuse-riddled problem of fatigue. Mornings, with freshness upon you, are usually best but for most of us errant souls, regularity is key.

The routine may be different for those whose writing is in the service of their occupations, but the principle is the same—to set time aside on a regular basis, even if during lunch hours, before or after work, in order to ensure you have written something. Don't put off that memo because you're afraid of it, as many are. Write while the notion is hot. Jot notes while your ideas are coming.

LET IDEAS JELL

Think them out in your subconscious mind—how marvelous intelligence is, two-tiered, as it were. Notions bubbling beneath will sooner or later bob to the surface.

Like the proverbial iceberg, only the tip shows—the bulk of the idea is concealed. Make sure you've thought it through before you set fingers on the keyboard. Consider all the details, and the ramifications. So only begin writing when you've mastered the details of the plot, the brief, the presentation, whatever. Then you'll feel mentally comfortable, which is important.

WORDS PER DAY

Produce not in bursts (like the sometime late-night writer) but in a steady stream, without falling off too far from what has been established, by trial and error, as normal output. Many writers have hewed to production schedules as if they were one-man factories. Norman Mailer once set a goal of seven pages a day, four days a week. Hemingway kept track on a chart of the words he wrote per day, about 500. Quotas may be helpful. Consider: If you can produce 1000 words a day, in 90 days—three months—you will have 90,000 words, a book. Doubtless, the revisions will take longer, but to get it down on paper is an excellent way to proceed.

Suppose you slept late, wrote for an hour, lunched, spent the afternoon gossiping or playing tennis, dined, watched TV, and messed around, but if in that single hour you produced a nearly perfect page, you'd have written a longish book at the end of the year. Unhappily, few of us have that facility. The good news is that solid work habits, once mastered, become almost second nature.

And it may be that an established work routine, as opposed to a flighty one, is a sign of growing up.

DAYS OFF

Do you suddenly become Catholic on Good Friday so you won't have to turn in your report? Are you a non-religious Jew who observes the Jewish holidays in order to stay home? Many want all the days off they can chisel, but the dedicated with *sitsfleysch* stick to their task.

Professional, self-employed writers are paid for

what they produce, whether it's a holiday or not. They often work a six-day week and put in an hour or so on Sunday to keep in practice—getting out of practice is all too easy—and to maintain momentum. They don't want to lose steam just because it's a weekend. On the other hand, because writing is so individual, you may need weekends off to reflect and refresh. But why should you conform to other people's calendars when you're free not to?

"Warning: Writing May Be Dangerous to Your Health"

The *sitsfleysch* system is designed to increase efficiency and if hard drugs accomplished that there might be reason for their use. But drugs produce the very opposite of total concentration, and if you believe they reward you with insights dredged from the depths, go back and read what you have written while under their thrall. Logic has almost certainly been lost.

Coffee, but not in excess, may be an aid. The French writer, Balzac, drank a dozen cups of Turkish coffee a day and apparently died as a result.

Nobody writes well drunk, although a cocktail at the end of the day may give you a certain distance from the page, as Joan Didion said, or may zap your flagging imagination and provide you with the last mile.

Writers who depend on their skills for a livelihood have an amazing faculty for rarely missing a day's work, unlike people who are paid when they stay home. Being unable to afford to be sick appears a remarkable tonic, one that health care professions should examine.

Obvious but true, good health aids writing; your physical condition affects your mind. And just as you should probably not write after big meals because your system is otherwise occupied, you shouldn't skip meals either. You need energy to concentrate and create. That requires eating, sleeping, and exercise. Don't be a flabby, pasty-faced writer. Now that you know how to sit down, stand up.

(If the exception proves the rule—a notion whose meaning I've never grasped—writers like Elizabeth Barrett Browning, the poet, and Charles Darwin, whose *On the Origin of Species* must be considered literature as well as science, did their work in bed.)

Step Three: The Right Idea

Picking, Plumbing, Planning

Writers of almost anything require ideas, even on how to elaborate a business proposal or compose a term paper. Suggestions on how to seize ideas and make the most of these sometimes elusive creatures.

Ideas, like butterflies, can come from any direction. To catch one, you need fast feet and a big net.

You can chase ideas by compiling lists of them (keep endless lists!), discarding those that don't pass muster, adding others until one clicks. (Click it will. You can almost hear the sound.) Often, purposeful observation is required—watch the world around you, read, listen, follow the news, decide what's interesting and useful, even though it might be no more than a chance remark you overheard. Be receptive not only to information and sensory data but to the crucial inner voice which, if you heed it, will whisper suggestions, sometimes at the strangest, most unexpected moments. (Precisely why the unconscious works as it does, in fits and starts, is not understood.)

Almost certainly, you've been dreaming up and storing ideas during your whole life, not excluding infancy. The trick is to tap the well and let them out. (One theory has it that, at least in some cases, a writer has a few initial perceptions even as a child and spends the rest of his career expressing and developing them.)

SOME THOUGHTS:

1. Provide yourself with a specific set of instructions about what you seek, much as you might program a computer. You can augment the flow by putting pressure on your psyche to produce, by telling it that you are ready to listen. Help your mind to work for you. Channel the psyche's energies in a purposeful manner. It may proceed in some mysterious fashion (unlike a computer) to free associate, to connect this with that and that with this, until from the womb of your mind, having gestated, an idea springs.

2. Keep an idea file. Don't throw ideas away. One

idea, even if unsuitable, may suggest another. What doesn't work on this occasion may serve brilliantly the next.

3. Avoid self-censorship. No easy task. Reflecting the need of our society to shield itself from pessimism, sadness, and grief, we have been drilled like soldiers in the ways of optimism and the power of positive thinking, so-called. Well and good, but there's a place, an important place, for looking at things with a cold eye. It may be that skeptical or "negative" thinking, as a counterweight to sloppy optimism, is healthy and positive in itself.

It takes effort—*sitsfleysch*—to pry from yourself insights that you as a writer can use. Approach in a spirit of candor.

Ideas abound: Consider that with a handful of notes composers can create new music without end. More difficult than inventing new ideas may be the selection of which to undertake. You might explore a dozen notions before finding one that appeals to you, is you, has what you want in it—social commentary, love, sex, novelty, humor, even practicality.

Generally, the longer the work projected the greater the forethought that should go into it if only because of the time to be spent. Why invest a year on a piece of writing only to discover the idea wasn't strong enough, or the project right for you?

For all the prethinking you've done, it's not always possible to know the outcome in advance, and you may have to experiment and give up part way through if you must. What writer has not? Judith Rossner and Erica Jong, to name two, write a hundred pages or more before deciding whether to proceed with a book. Most writers have unpublished material.

It must be stressed that the brain is not a precision instrument. The mind can't always provide on cue what you seek. It must be aided, coddled, trained like a muscle, by, well, your inner force. Do not expect quantum leaps. Proceed in tiny steps, one at a time, like evolution.

SUBJECT MATTER

Given the variety of ideas at your disposal today and the difficulties of being published, it make sense for most writers to avoid subjects of only marginal interest.

This caution is neither a cop-out or sellout. On whatever level of your aspiration, if idea (A) is as good as idea (B), but (B) will appeal only to the owners of tawny Siamese cats while (A) will thrill every cat lover, (A) is the logical choice. Of course, if you burn to write about tawny Siamese cats, nobody can stop you. (Sigh.)

In analyzing the intrinsic appeal of a subject, it's no crime to imagine the potential audience. For instance, I imagine some of you as eager, "creative," lazy sometimes, and more than a little frustrated at your lack of *sitsfleysch*. I see some of you as wanting or needing to write better on the job, others as content with being Sunday writers, and others as longing to write for a living as an independent, a freelance, a professional, but feeling underqualified. You fear you lack "genius," but John Gardner points to the "secret emptiness" of that phrase. Everyone has some genius. It's parcelled out among us like the light, though some may shine brighter than others.

"Creative" and "Commercial"

You may think, or have been told, that what you write or want to write isn't "creative." But what does or doesn't merit the label depends on who's deciding what "creative" is. Don't be hung up on such clichés.

"Creative religion," "creative sex," "creative gardening"—"creative creativity" would no longer seem impossible. The word "creative" has been wrenched out of shape by being put in so many contexts as to become an improvisation but it has enough edge left so that accusations as to its absence can hurt.

Keep in mind during the idea-forming stages that "creative" is often used arbitrarily and weighted in favor of "liberal" arts. To prepare a technical manual, a set of instructions, a business letter, or a seed catalogue can't be described as creative writing (though clarity, originality, and attractiveness will reflect creativity). But much writing not normally thought of in such terms can be called creative: Presentations, annual reports, term papers and dissertations, speeches, promotional literature. All manner of material that requires active writing should qualify as "creative."

Similarly, "commercial" is often employed unevenly, even with disparagement, as if only hacks are paid. So don't worry about being "creative" or "commercial."

Research

Pondered, your idea not only passes mental muster but your never-to-be neglected instincts tell you that it's right. The inner pressure to produce grows. Still, you may feel you need to know more about the subject, and holding back a little might be wise. It usually is.

In nonfiction especially (but very often in fiction, too) research is a requirement. Under the *sitsfleysch* system it ought to be done as economically as possible or you will be lost forever in the maze of facts and flood tide of academic trivia our society busily accumulates.

It's smart at the outset to make an overall survey of the field, as with an aerial camera. Establish the pertinent areas. Decide, if you can, what research you don't need. When information begins to repeat itself, you probably have enough, to start with at least.

As one writer put it, "When I meet myself coming out of a tunnel, I know I've done enough research."

Printed Material

Support your public library! Use it! For all the fanfare given to electronic data bases, computers can't accomplish everything and libraries are a lot cheaper.

Find relevant books in the library card catalogue. *Books in Print*, *The Reader's Guide to Periodical Material*, *Sociological Abstracts*, and other indices will steer you to appropriate magazine and journal articles. That nice librarian will help. A reference librarian may be willing to undertake a search for you, although sometimes for a fee.

Many libraries are depleted of books and publications because immoral people have lifted them, depriving others, and the libraries don't have the money to replace them even when they can. Stores specializing in out-of-print and backdated books may have them. Book sellers specializing in out-of-print books are listed geographically in *American Book Trade Directory*. The *New York Times Book Review*, and other literary periodicals, list out-of-print book dealers who, if they do not have the book, will try to obtain it for you. The Library of Congress collects every book printed in the U.S., if you can manage a trip to Washington. Many libraries, especially those of universities, are part of an interlibrary loan system and can get you books from around the area. Newspapers have files of their back issues on microfilm and microfiche, but, naturally, they only cover themselves.

COMPUTER BANKS

There are thousands of them, usually organized by a kind of information retailer. What is going on in the post-electronic era is utterly amazing and has great relevance to the writer. Never before has information been so plentiful and easily available. It would have taken years of effort, or more than a lifetime, or been impossible, to ferret out the sources the computer can instantly provide, from publications around the world, usually in abstracts. Writers can know more than previous writers if they choose.

Still, a caution: Because everything has been thrown into the computer pot, you have to be careful about what you order, since you pay for it. The labeling of abstracts is sometimes inadequate. (See Data Bases.)

EXPERTS

A shortcut may be to use experts to guide you. Experts may have the answers or know others who do. And they may possess the printed materials you need. Don't be shy about contacting experts: They're often flattered to be called and surprisingly generous with time if they're convinced you're serious. You can find experts in the govemment, on campuses, in businesses, sometimes even on your own block. You can check the Yellow Pages. (Suppose you want to know about lumber. Call a lumber yard.)

PLACES

In fiction particularly, you may want exotic locales, but you don't have to leave home. Some of those detailed descriptions you've read in bestsellers come from other books, travel guides, and the author's imagination. But you must sound authentic, the skill of an author like Tom Clancy.

You, Too, Are a Resource

Your notes may be research—observations (the shape of a car or a tree), metaphors you've thought of, character sketches for fiction, suggestions to yourself how to proceed. Random jottings can be highly important, since they may provide valuable intuitive leads you will later follow.

"I saw the most remarkable nose today on the street. It was long, sharp as a blade, and mottled. The nose belonged to a person, of course (a man), but suppose it hadn't? Being only a nose in the air. Story idea?"

You might carry a small tape recorder in which to store your thoughts. You might want several notebooks, one for the "work in progress" (that gallant graduate-school phrase), others for future projects. As always under the *sitsfleysch* system, plan well ahead.

You can also keep the notes on index cards, alphabetized or otherwise categorized in a box, or stored in a word processor. Later on, when writing, you'll find it easier to locate a fact or an insight.

Step Four: The Write Stuff

The acid test: writing itself. The ski slope.
Application of fiction to nonfiction. Style.
Imitation.

The capacity to sit down for prolonged periods and to develop ideas is hardly the whole story. Writing is an active task that requires both concentration and energy. It is difficult, frustrating, and demanding. With that in mind, you begin.

It's not like starting a machine—you can't just press a switch. You must ORGANIZE because in writing, organization is everything and everything is organization, or ought to be if the work is to proceed. Don't worry about overorganizing, either. Your precious spark will survive and burn more brightly.

Organization doesn't mean sorting paper clips, but making as many decisions as possible in advance, including your method. Not doing so can make you pay dearly later on.

EARLY ANALYSIS

It is essential at the outset to have an overall vision. Professional writers do this automatically but they do it all the same.

One early decision which may seem obvious but could be the major cause of a miscarriage is the form to work in: Exposition ("nonfiction" sounds as though fiction were king instead of a poor relative to factual writing), play, TV or film script, article, essay, short fiction, novel, and so on. Elementary as it may seem, the point is raised because it is all too easy to go wrong—the novel that should have been a short story or (occasionally) vice versa, the film script that should have been a one act play, the full blown report that might have been a longish memo.

You have to know yourself as well. Many writers can be compared to runners—there are distances at which each may excel. Some are natural sprinters who write best at short length articles, stories, vignettes, while others are milers who write books, or marathon runners who write long books. Some writers can handle anything. Give thought as to the length you feel comfortable with, or will have to train up to.

Publishers seem to prefer long books as though writers were paid by the pound.

The amount of planning depends on the individual, but writers who begin with an empty head and blank pages are all too likely to end with same.

The Outline

Unless it's a short take that doesn't require one, prepare an outline, partly to corroborate that what you're about to undertake is do-able and worth doing, and partly to chart the virgin territory you're about to enter. You're an explorer and you need to make a map as you go. Be wary of omitting this crucial step; it may be your hardest task.

How detailed the outline should be varies, of course, from writer to writer and project to project. Perhaps you will be able to encapsulate an idea on a single page (sufficient length for a magazine article proposal, divided into three or four succinct points), or perhaps you'll need ten pages or more to communicate fully (and commune with yourself).

In fact, the outline, if fully developed, is essentially the book you plan to write and the basis of what the publisher pays you in advance.

The outline ought to proceed from start to finish and include a middle—otherwise you'll have a head and tail but no body. Beginning writers, especially, are apt to think that a flashy opening and a strong climax are enough, but if the center won't hold neither will the rest. That's where *sitsfleysch* comes in—to develop the theme carefully before starting to write.

It's probably sensible to have a working title, an idea of deeper significance than may appear. Some writers wait for the right title to flash like lightning, or leap at them from the text, but to veer off theme is astonishingly easy (even in business and professional writing). An advance title that seems the core of what you want to say will keep the imperfect brain on track and maintain your focus. Tape the title to a wall and stare at it when in doubt about the next move. You can always change the title later.

In the outline you may proceed slowly from point to point, event to event, or you may apply, even at this preliminary stage, the Russian writer Isaac Babel's dictum to "write with fire and correct with phlegm." If so, don't worry when your stream-of-consciousness (or unconsciousness) has eddies and whirlpools—let if flow and fix afterward. You may even end with two outlines, a long one for your own use and a polished shortened version to show an editor, boss, or agent.

I happen to have a particularly fussy one. "Nothing leaves this office unless it's perfect," he says, and it's not unusual for him to bounce an outline back to me, with suggestions, three or four times. Ruefully, I accept the ideas when good, and try again.

How closely you stay with the plan in the actual writing is up to you, of course. It's not a blueprint: You're free to alter it as new insights and information decree. But you have a scheme.

Let's take a few steps back before proceeding. We laid down a few rules regarding the writer's environment and psychology and then discussed the stages preliminary to actual writing. The first was the idea, which we can now define as inspiration. The second, somewhat distinct from it, was conception, the careful planning, through early analysis, research and outline, of what is to be attempted.

Adequate care will make the next step, execution, that much easier.

To Start With

That blank page can be a harrowing experience—an expanse of white sneering at you, challenging your ability to cross it, announcing (except for a short letter or poem) it's only one of more to follow, many more in the case of a book.

But you don't have to start with page one—you can begin in the middle and jump around as notions occur and the material beckons, threading the sections together later, as many writers do—Vladamir Nabokov was one. Still, no matter where it comes to rest, it's still the first page that you write.

Dorothea Brande recommends a series of Zen-like exercises to quell apprehension, or you might fall back on what we'll call:

THE SKI-SLOPE PRINCIPLE

After you've checked the route, don't look at the whole mountain but only at the next stretch. This technique may be for cowards but the prospect of having to complete dozens or hundreds of blank pages can be unsettling to any sane mind.

The self-programming referred to earlier may also be an aid. You inform yourself that by day "X" you'll be ready: On day "X" you begin.

Skiers ought to warm up and so might you by dashing off verse and even a short letter (remember letters?), anything to flex the fingers and limber the head. You could read a little, play around with the voice, the tone in which you'll address the reader. ("Voice" also applies to some extent to business communications.) Experiment with style to hear what variations carry the voice best. Practice, as the pianist would with scales.

Try this: Describe a cat. Just a cat in general. Now, repeat the effort, in one paragraph, only make it a specific cat. Read it over, and insert whatever details you realize you've left out. Is it a real cat? Does it have cattiness? If so, you've succeeded.

You may not be aware but you've already begun to write, though the first page remains empty. (If you're superstitious, you won't number the page until after you've finished it.)

There! The first sentence has landed. It may be a limp sentence and probably is, but by the time you've rewritten it, the second sentence is ready in your mind and so on, until you've achieved a paragraph. It may be a rotten paragraph, but by the time you've rewritten it, it'll be better.

A teacher named Paul Pierog gives a writing course in New York City he calls "Wordspace." He advises his students, some quite young, as follows:

"With people and objects, we basically go through two steps: first we focus on how far we can take the single item of the focus; then we concentrate on concretely constructing it in a singular place with language."

This is a boy. He is about one year old. He has blue and very expressive eyes. He is happy now and his eyes smile and sparkle. Next minute he begins to think about something very important to him because his eyes become very serious and lubrication shows on his child's face. Unexpectedly a barely noticeable shadow covers his face. He knits his brows. His blue eyes become dark and a sea of tears fill them. The first big tear

rolls down his cheek. He is crying.
Through the tears he sees a bird which
sits near the window and his eyes smile
again.

(Mariya Dushkina)

Similarly, business writing should be done with
flair, but you need words on paper. Put them down,
sentence by sentence, until you've achieved a
memo. Is it awkward, ungainly, contrived, long-
winded? Or does it have the essentials of a good
memo? Has it got memoness?* If so, you've done
your job.

Early on, you should decide on your speed. Some
writers race through the original draft, as if afraid a
beast is behind them, before returning to correct.
This is the boldest course, and the advantage is
indubitable—to pull it out of you while you are
enthusiastic and energetic. Still, safer and safety, as
a high-wire acrobat's net provides, is important
because to crash may be discouraging if not fatal.

You may want to write twenty such satisfactory
pages (in the case of a book) to set the standard and
voice for what will follow. You're establishing your
credentials, informing yourself that you have won

---

*Memoness: April was a tough month for TIME International, with only $6.1 million
in ad revenue added vs. $9.2 million in 1985. Our superior bookings performance
throughout the first quarter, largely fueled by the international lotteries, has essentially
flattened. TIME International now stands just $2.4 million ahead of last year's booking
level, an increase of 5%. We were 13.6 ahead one month ago. Area Director's estimates
total $91.5 million vs. $85.6 actual in 1985.

A positive point to be noted: We have booked 2,182 pages in the first half against
2,058 last year. This represents a major step toward reversing a three year decline in volume. Each edition, with the exception of Asia, is ahead in pages booked year to date.

the right to a reader's attention. At some point you may wish to write with fire, as the urge hits, but when? Never, maybe. You may find it surer to be methodical throughout, because you'll be nearer the mark and will need fewer corrections.

STRUCTURING

It's usually convenient, if not essential, to organize your projected work into sections—chapters in the case of a book. And it may well be, at least in the outline (pre-actual-writing) stage, to imagine them as of more or less equal length. This will tend to distribute the weight more equally.

You might begin by dividing the material into major sections—Part I, Part II, Part III. Then you can subdivide into parcels—Chapter I, Chapter II...etc.

"In Chapter Six (you write) my heroine, Lonnie, begins to suspect that her interest in Jim, her second cousin who broke his arm rescuing her in the accident, is more than casual. Bringing Lonnie around is a combination of circumstances, especially the one involving the sailboat..."

What's obvious is that sections which should be organized in arresting ways all too often aren't. Ingredients that should have produced interesting results turn out dull because the author failed to stir the pot or gave up too soon. The right sequence structure may be key.

That advice clearly applies to dramatic material but has application to the non-dramatic as well. Your long report may be far more effective if the pieces of it are so arranged as to build to a climax, as a novel should.

THE TEXT

It's really fairly simple at this stage: Page follows page as you stick to (or for cogent reasons, depart from) the outline, observing your *sitsfleysch* schedule, taking breaks when you need to but always returning to your desk until the appointed hour when you stop.

Hemingway's priceless advice was not to quit until you know exactly how you'll begin the next day, down perhaps to precise words. The reason is obvious: If you start cold, you'll have to build momentum once more. Again, simple.

Nothing, of course, is simple about writing. Well—I never promised you a prose garden. The decisions a writer has to make in the course of a memo or manuscript, especially a long one, are past counting. How many possibilities exist in the selection of 100,000 right words for a book? To say nothing of making sentences, forming transitions, breaking ideas down into paragraphs, sections and chapters, deploying material for dramatic effect, of changing pace to keep readers interested, of spelling, punctuation....

Don't Stop

You knew in advance that you'd become discouraged: Remember that and persevere. Hackneyed as it sounds, persistence may succeed where "genius" fails. Again, it's not unlike running. Because of fatigue you want to give up but if you press on, you break through the barrier.

Floundering Around

At the same time, a foolish persistence can be the hobgoblin of little writers who fail to recognize that flexibility is required too. If something doesn't work, stop, look, and listen. Ask what's wrong, test the approach, go another way. Writers must flounder. Persistence shouldn't be confused with bullheadedness. Don't batter at the gates. If a presentation, paper, or proposal, seems to be stiff, disjointed, unpersuasive or unattractive for all your efforts, test it another way. If your article appears to lack immediacy and vitality, use another angle. If you can't write convincingly about sex, minimize or avoid it. (In fiction, sexual allusions are preferable more often than not to explicit detail.) If characterizations are a problem, concentrate more on narrative. Consider descriptions when the action drags.

If your transitions are clumsy, see what happens when you lop off the last sentence of a paragraph.

If you're repetitious, take down *Webster's New Dictionary of Synonyms*, *Roget's Thesaurus*, *Brewer's Dictionary of Phrase and Fable*, *Fowler's*.

You may find that reference books will steer you around the shoals of language and composition. Dictionaries, rhyming dictionaries, dictionaries of synonyms, guides to style—they were prepared for writers like you. Have them in your library. Also, poetry may help.

Be direct, as you would be in conversation. If you back into the subject, you probably begin too slowly.

"Nothing puts the reader off more than a great slab of prose at the start," said the novelist P.G. Wodehouse, a remark that applies to all sorts of writing. Don't over-explain. The habit, especially for beginning writers, is to throw into the pot every pet theory they have but, for the most part, gratuitous observations should be dropped.

"While acts never become obsolete or stale, commentaries always do," remarks Isaac Bashevis Singer, winner of the Nobel Prize.

It may be that your material has inherent difficulties that you feel you lack the ability to solve. Innovate, improvise, employ artifice. In the Parthenon, facing steps seem perfectly symmetrical. Only if you examine closely will you see that the sets of steps are quite different. Brilliant Greek architects achieved harmony by deceiving the eye.

So, shortcomings—and all writers have them in one degree or another (pet words that are repeated too often, for instance)—don't have to be fatal and probably aren't. Coaches help athletes by concentrating on their skills to compensate for their weaknesses. Do what you do best, and perhaps only what you do best.

REINFORCEMENT

You should check to see if your ideas are sufficiently developed. That is, backed up by enough acts, illustrations, descriptions, and so on. As a learning experience, take some magazines—*The New Yorker* and *Reader's Digest*, for instance—and analyze the major ideas in an article, encircling them. Then measure the space between the principal thoughts. That material is usually reinforcement. (Oddly, perhaps, *The New Yorker* provides a great deal of that. The *New York Review of Books* uses very little.)

FICTION—AND SOME APPLICATIONS

The usual distinction between fiction and nonfiction has not been observed here because the writing process is the same.

Of course, fiction and nonfiction have obvious differences, but as we explore fiction, bear this in mind: Fiction may be the more interesting form because it requires so much inventiveness. The storyteller works hard to attract your attention and make you believe him or her. Many fictional techniques can be usefully applied to other sorts of writing.

The burden for the fiction writer is realism, almost as if the reader musn't be let in on the secret that he's reading fiction. Quirkiness, too many embellishments, awkward slips that expose the tale as having been invented, must not be allowed. The reader has to be brought inside the story, so that he senses himself sitting on the furniture, looking out.

Realistic detail is crucial because the audience wants to learn something in fiction so as not to waste time. It likes information, the more complete the better, or how things work, be it spies, psychoanalysis, or starting a fire. Many fiction writers have to learn how to use facts.

One skill of an accomplished fiction writer is to make information vivid. It can be stodgy, as in a census, or it can be placed in contexts where it springs from the page.

"Marsupials in Michigan," is far less arresting than "Kangaroos in Kalamazoo."

Or this, from Paul Pierog's writing class:

Ceiling

by
Keith Harris

The lower ceiling was white with tiny black polka dots. The tiles were sectioned off in squares, but it didn't seem to be in any uniformed pattern. In the center of the ceiling was a fluorescent light fixture with four bulbs. Two of the bulbs were burnt out and I could hear a slight buzzing sound. In the corner was a water spot which had turned the ceiling tiles muddy brown. Twelve of the tiles seemed ready to collapse. This was a ceiling in need of repair. It was bordered by cheap wood, rough to the touch. Smudgy hand prints on four of the tiles seemed to be supporting this dilapidated ceiling with some unknown force. A concern for my safety prompted me to make a hasty exit.

In a memo, term paper, a report, an article, whatever, make the reader sit up. Surprise him (or her—how I long for an all-gender word that would satisfy everyone).

To outline fiction requires skill and *sitsfleysch* in

abundance. The decisive elements are the plot, the characters, and the point of view. Although the story is usually one you invent or embellish on, it cannot be completely arbitrary. On however deep a level, it must conform to a picture of the world the reader already has in his head.

All this also applies to a paper, a memo, and a business letter. That a presentation has a beginning, a middle and an end is not merely an obvious formal rule but one that seems to correspond to the workings of the mind.

In fiction, the beginning not only starts to explain the problems you are about to encounter, but tries to attract you in with a question, a tickler.

"Unhappy families are all alike. Happy families are all different, each in its own way," commences *War and Peace*. With a seeming paradox, Tolstoy grabs your attention at once.

So should, within reason, a business letter, a political speech, a sociological dissertation. That they often don't reflects the lack of imaginative approach.

In fiction, the middle is an expansion, an elucidation, of the theme or themes laid down at the start. That is why it is most important to get the original elements right. Then, the development can be shown in a systematic, though dramatic, manner.

Successful "middles" are hard to do in fiction because the action tends to lag; the same can be said about business and professional written material whose interest may decline after the opening remarks. George Santayana, the philosopher, complained that long poems were often inferior to short ones because the longer poems weren't worked on hard enough. Work hard at your middle.

The fictional resolution, the outcome, in a skillful writer's hands becomes virtually inevitable even if a nonsolution is arrived at—"options" as they say. (Writers who use "options" aren't aware of the difference between "alternatives"—two—and "choices"—more than two.) The choices the characters have must be presented convincingly. Walking off into the sunset will not normally suffice—unless it's the last sunset.

It's wise to decide on the ending before you arrive there, before you start, if possible. Nothing ruins a novel more easily than a disappointing conclusion. Your readers may have been immersed throughout but if you let them down in the last ten pages, they'll judge it a bad book. It might have been a very good book except you ran out of *sitsfleysch* in the last chapter.

In nonfiction, too, the ending may be vital. It is, maybe, the last chance to "clinch the deal," to convince, to impress. Make your exit memorable. Wrap it up with a sense of invincibility and daring. Leave your audience begging for more. Your next entrance will be easier.

The plot can be as twisty and convoluted as you like. If it seems thin, you may require an underplot, a sort of sub-basement to the main story where another set of events unfold, though eventually all must come together. You are free to move backward and forward in time although, often, a writer who needs flashbacks may not have been able to integrate information within the narrative, through dialogue, for instance. Flashbacks can be a bore.

These notions have applicability to standard communications, too. You have to move the argument along, as quickly and with as few redundancies (flashbacks) as possible. Lay it out like an action narrative. That (and what doesn't that's decent?) takes work. Lawyers would do well to read good novels as models for their briefs.

Most novels are built with scenes which can be thought of as jewels in a watch, when watches had jewels. The plot often turns around major scenes, and you should determine at least some of them in advance so as not to flounder more than you already will. An artist's sketchbook, with large pages, can be of assistance. Describe the scene in a few words, circle it, and connect it with arrows to other scenes.

That may be a hint for ordinary written communication, too. When you seek to attract the attention of your reader, you might consider paragraphs as scenes and lay them out as a novelist would, with the longer, stronger ones arranged to emphasize their importance.

Should the characters be modeled on real people?

Practitioners of fiction have to understand how to foreshadow (dropping hints, clues or references, to what will happen later) so that the reader won't be surprised and will feel comfortable with a new character or plot development. To some extent, that goes for other kinds of writing as well. Set the stage for the next argument or proposition.

One person you should probably not base a character on is yourself. Autobiographical novels usually don't work because the writer loses perspective when leading the cast. Otherwise, to pattern appearances, traits, characteristics or even whole personalities after living individuals you've encountered—or montages of them—can be of use. In any case, to make the characters believable, you will naturally fall back on copying real people. They're all you know. (Science fiction writers sometimes err by trying to imagine personalities which have little or no relation to earthlings. They cannot, and will be unable to, until an extraterrestrial personality appears as a model. The frequent result for science fiction is weak characterizations.)

I don't wish to reduce the point to absurdity, but character can play a role, even in a classified ad. The lady has a dog. She finds she has an allergy to dog hair and must get rid of it. How does the ad read? "Puppy for sale"? or, conveying the dog's nature: "Little black ball, name it as you want, has one white whisker, a love for laps, and unlimited licks. The darling pooch is, unhappily, for sale."

A cold eye is needed as well as a warm one in molding characters. When we perceive other people truly, we see a highly complex mix of personality traits, some of which we like and some of which we don't. Is this enormous differentiation genetically based, nature's effort (like our faces and bodies) to keep us distinct and provide evolutionary possibilities? We often wish people were different, but even a writer of fiction understands that after a point, personality is irreducible. He sticks in his knife and when he hits a hard place, he's onto character that's formed and will be resistant to alteration. Still, even if only a small part of your fictional person will or can change, small changes can loom large in life, and the writer of good fiction aims to have his main characters different at the end from what they were at the beginning, with the story supplying the reasons. (Ask yourself, when reading a potboiler, whether the characters change.)

Though you may long to (and maybe you can, after all) you can't change the character of the individual who is reading your analysis or report. But you may be able to influence other people's views, and you want to make your own persona, as revealed by what you write, such that others will be compelled to listen. To convince them, you may have to understand who they are and allow them to understand who you are. Gaining support for your position by implicitly expressing your own character is completely normal and requires understanding of the others involved. (Not for nothing do we call people "characters.")

Individuals are, in the end, themselves, and there is little that they or you can do about it. Short of putting them into psychotherapy, you must take them as they are, for better or worse. The same can be said for fictional characters. When you've reached the stage that even you, their creator, can't make them act in ways they won't want to, then they have a life of their own.

Once you've given birth to characters, be loyal to them—they're your children. To you they are real. Ask yourself how they would act in this or that situation. Believe in them as though they existed—if you don't, nobody else will either.

NAMES

In fiction, characters will have to be christened, so why not get a jump? Pluck names out of phone books. Keep a list of those that appeal to you. Usually, if you imagine a character and let your mind wander, a name that suggests what you want to convey will come. And names can be important. If a name resonates for you it may for the reader. Charles Dickens had absolute mastery in choosing names like David Copperfield that perfectly fit his character and himself. ("D.C."—"C.D." reversed?) So did Nabokov with Humbert Humbert in *Lolita*.

Don't people, oddly, seem to conform to what they are called? Of course, you are named by your parents, who had a position in time and society and, consciously or not, selected your name as part of their expectations for you—expectations which you in some degree probably share. (Sharon, the beauty, David, the wise.) It is no different in fiction: You are the parent of your characters, so take good care in naming them, no matter how badly they wind up.

TRUE CRIME

True or fact, crime writing is, at its best, a crossbreed of non-fiction and fiction, and poses a number of challenges. The non-fiction part is to explain the crime (usually murder) and how it was solved. You will need a time-line such as the detectives used, or the time-line they established. A skilled detective is often an excellent judge of personality. (A tip: if you're about to tackle a true crime, establish friendships with detectives; be sure they trust you and that the trust is merited.)

Now comes the fiction part. Suspense. Creating suspense is often integral to fiction. You have to raise questions at the outset, and you will need an opening scene or scenes—the discovery of a body, a missing person—that evokes mystery. Then, as in fiction, you must develop the important characters you will string like beads throughout the story.

Your story should contain elements of surprise. Perhaps the forensics, perhaps the trial, perhaps your lead detective's remarkable ingenuity (or persistence) in nabbing the culprit. Still, the key to success in the fact-crime genre is realism, as provided by endless details. Your research must provide them.

Remember: in fiction and non-fiction, you're always headed toward a conclusion, gathering momentum as you go. Every move should be directed toward that objective like the end game in chess, only here the opponent might be yourself. Think of the first sentence as a prelude to the last, and know where you are every step of the way. This advice is easy to give and hard to follow.

DIALOGUE

Your people, being such, will tend to talk. Some fiction writers claim dialogue is the hardest part, some the easiest, which may be a matter of how much they rely on and practice it. Individuals are usually shortwinded (except on the phone). If you keep your dialogue short, too, the writing of it will be simpler. Try writing down or recording snippets of conversations you hear to give yourself a better idea of how people actually speak. Listen for word choice and dissimilarities of voice.

POV

Just as you should strive to keep a balance among plot, settings and characterizations, so you should follow the rules in fiction regarding point of view—"POV" as denoted in film scripts for where the camera points. Understanding POV is essential, or ought to be: Even writers who parade on the best-seller list sometimes don't have the hang of it, with the result that the reader is jolted into disbelief. Rarely can you deviate successfully from the POV you've established.

POV in fiction means who's telling the story and there are, essentially, three possible approaches: First person singular ("I"), third person singular ("he" or "she") and the omniscient or universal narrator who sees all. Each POV has advantages and drawbacks. There are no free lunches in writing either, unless you're the speaker at a book-and-author function.

The main advantage of the omniscient approach is that it's the easiest to handle. That's the major reason so many writers select it. The universal narrator knows all and can enter a character's head any time he chooses. The drawback of the technique (all writing is technique) is that it can be shallow, distracting, and uneven. In the hands of a master, however, it is a fine approach.

First person singular narration is, ordinarily, the most difficult to achieve because "au" (as proofreaders designate authors) is compelled to relate and describe everything through the eyes of "I"—nothing can happen that "I" doesn't know about, and this means the writer must compress every event into a single perspective and finesse those who refuse to fall within that context. (In *Sophie's Choice*, Styron used a one-step remove from the first person singular, an "I" narrator who tells someone else's story.)

A compromise between these two POVs is the third person singular, which allows for the continuity of a single perspective yet gives the writer latitude to describe things on his own, without the blinders of "I," even though "he" or "she" may not get as close to the bone as "I" can. It's also possible to have two third person singular points of view, as represented by two characters through whose eyes the story is told in alternating chapters, say. But if two's company, three's a crowd that demands the omniscient point of view.

The POV ought to be carefully and deliberately selected, even experimented with, in terms of the needs of the material. Do it in advance to avoid the self-loathing that can result from squandering hours and *sitsfleysch*. (Some writers evidently believe in eternal life, so profligate are they with time.) But whatever the POV, and the difficulty of forcing the action into a particular frame, stay within it.

Ordinary business communication ought to abide by the laws of POV, too. If you're writing as though the company is speaking, don't switch to the first person. If you're writing as the spokesperson for someone else, don't go into the universal mode. If you're writing as yourself, don't bootleg the organization's authority.

ON STYLE

Can style be learned? If not, it can certainly be improved.

You will have, and probably have already since you speak (whether writing is based on speech or vice versa is a matter of academic debate) a style of your own, but insofar as you're developing it (a writer always should be), make it simple.

"Good writers are those who keep the language efficient. That is to say, keep it accurate, keep it clear," advised the poet Ezra Pound.

Don't be blowsy and overblown. Steer away from the "fog factor"—incomprehensibility wrought by unwieldy paragraphs and interminable sentences studded with difficult words. Between "quotidian" and "daily," use "daily" unless "quotidian" has solid reasons for being there. That's not to say that "big" words should always be avoided. They exist for a reason—they may communicate shades of meaning. Without them, the language would be impoverished. We think in words, and, if words are depleted, we may remove nuances or subtleties in thinking.

HANG-UPS

Writers can have verbal hang-ups, words they repeat without being aware. (I know, I know, mine is "it.") Make a list of words you repeat and avoid them.

Just the same, don't be overly frightened of repetition. Some writers pore through the thesaurus in search of synonyms to add variety. Take the word "love." I...love, like enjoy, dote on, *or* in, relish, fancy, adore, worship, idolize, cherish, treasure, value, prize...*Webster's Dictionary of Synonyms* suggests, but too many synonyms may sound affected. Sometimes it's better, if not vital to understanding, to employ the same word.

Generally, the idea "small is beautiful" applies to writing if you substitute "short" for small. This goes for words, sentences and paragraphs.

Some writers believe it's good to make the reader reach for the dictionary and add to his storehouse of words. Maybe so, but the danger is you'll interrupt the flow and distract the reader, maybe fatally.

Short sentences, therefore, give the illusion, at least, of being simple and easy to absorb, and illusions may be important. Don't let the reader feel overwhelmed. Whether he or she knows it or not, the reader will scan to get an advance impression if the text is difficult and, therefore, to be avoided. You do not want to throw them off.

You might believe only beginning writers learn from other writers, but it isn't true. Good, seasoned writers study each other's work, and are not afraid to borrow.

"Lesser artists imitate, great ones plagiarize," said Oscar Wilde; and the critic Lionel Trilling paraphrased him: "Immature artists imitate. Mature artists steal." He was only partly joking.

In any case, you may want to stop from time to time and check your work against established writers to see how yours measures up.

You have to read. Writers who don't continue to read generally won't write well. Standards must be refreshed, imagination inspired. Read!

(Since writing does or should mean reading, improve your reading skills. If you're slow, learning to read faster isn't all that hard. There are courses and books on the subject, but one easy method is to read a page in quarters—top left, bottom left, top right, bottom right—to absorb the ideas quickly. One of the better preparations for reading better, circuitous as it may seem, is writing better. You learn to probe another writer's mind.)

The imitation—or stealing—of technique can be helpful but don't imitate to the point of copying, don't imitate writers in translation, don't imitate idiosyncratic writers, no matter how splendid—

Nabokov, Faulkner, Joyce, Hemingway (whose seemingly simple style was related to poetry), Vonnegut and so on. They may affect you adversely and you may have to laboriously delearn in order to find your own voice.

Graham Greene is an exceptionally good model because of his clarity, perfect composition, and absence of literary hoke. Writers might do well to keep a copy of *The Human Factor* on their desks to see how well they measure up to it or to his autobiography, *A Sort of Life*. Robert Stone also sets an excellent standard.

Study writing that employs active verbs, avoids exaggeration, that's smooth, moves swiftly yet with emotion—in nonfiction, the later Tom Wolfe, for instance, or Jonathan Schell's *The Fate of the Earth*, an effective polemic that first appeared in *The New Yorker*. *The New Yorker* is a wonderful example of consistent style, though you don't have to like it. One big New York advertising agency gives a year's subscription to every copy trainee who walks in the door. Still, be careful. *The New Yorker* is highly specialized and can be a deceptive model.

Writers who emphasize their style, like Thomas Mann, Saul Bellow, or Norman Mailer, are difficult to emulate. (Think of Joe DiMaggio, who made hard catches look easy, unlike today's baseball entertainers, who turn pop flies into a production number.) Try a style-of-no-style, simple, direct, unobtrusive, relaxed, whose main function is not to call attention to itself so that the reader isn't aware of reading.

As the poet W.H. Auden said, "The test of good prose is that the reader does not notice it any more than a man looking through a window at a landscape notices the glass; if he does, it means the window is dirty."

To achieve those "clear windows" of prose requires plenty of polishing and *sitsfleysch*. Easy reading springs from hard writing. What Mann meant by "The writer is the person for whom writing is more difficult than for others," is that the writer has higher standards and has to work to achieve them.

The basic building blocks of writing are sentences, and to write a straightforward declarative sentence with the values it should contain is no minor accomplishment. To return to the comparison of runners, writers may have natural sentence lengths, some to shorter, some to longer ones, and if it's too great an effort for a long-sentence writer to handle short sentences, he should stay in his own stride. Nonetheless, he should be prepared to cut.

A sentence is strong when it feels strong, when it captures your intention in the fullest possible way. Like the language it's written in, the sentence replicates the process of thinking, and the better the sentence the better the thought that went into it. One reason writing well is tough is because the mind is filled with chatter and static, and it must decide which verbal order has to be established. If you can organize your thoughts, you automatically organize your writing. This is true for fiction and non.

Step Five: Read It and Weep

On revisions, accepting advice, clichés and other potent matters.

Was the agony worth it? Not if you don't take the time and work required to bring your material into its final, polished form, and that can be painful as hell, requiring endless rereading. The sportswriter Red Smith was right.

"There's nothing to writing," Smith said. "All you do is sit down and open a vein."

Who compels you to trample on paper fields you've so carefully tilled? Your inner critic. An inner critic is a must.

How do you develop and utilize the inner critic—a helpful one, not one that fills you with guilt?

With introspection, experimentation, using your taste, tapping your deepest thoughts.

Writing can be looked at as construction. Notes are the foundation, the outline is the frame, and the drafts are the interior. Editing is the facade, and in the final version you will undoubtedly subtract things, eliminating the irrelevant.

NOT ENOUGH REVISION

Revision, re-vision, after all, means to see again.

Have you padded too heavily? Have you reinforced too much?

Novelist Jack Kerouac wrote endlessly on one long Western Union paper roll, the proof being the defects. Sidney Sheldon says he writes a dozen drafts of a novel. Some writers of short stories complete dozens of drafts, dozens. Even if it's only a memo or a paper, get it right. Tighten, add, subtract, delete repetitions and redundancies, polish, flesh (*sitsfleysch*) out. Find words that are more appropriate. Edit. You know you're on track when you finally see that your favorite phrase or passage—the one you sweated over, were so proud to have—doesn't fit the context and must be filed away. Some suggest letting your production "cool" for a week or so before you go over it again.

And it may be profitable to show your work to others.

ADVICE

You may well be uncertain about a notion or how ably you've handled an idea, but when you seek advice, ask only those you respect and will listen to.

"Keep your own counsel," the writer may sometimes be warned because if you discuss your ideas you'll be talked out of them or they'll lose their force and become stale. Guard your ideas like military secrets, is cautioned; don't even discuss them.

"I just think it's bad to talk about the present work," said Norman Mailer, "for it spoils something at the root of the creative act. It discharges the tension."

But if your concept is so frail that it can't withstand scrutiny, if you lose the tension and tire of a notion as easily as that, perhaps it should be allowed to fade away. If it's not worthwhile, or plain silly, you should be told. Unlike scientists, who operate in teams, writers don't generally have colleagues to confer with and it's all too easy for them to wander into a bog. To see where you've gone wrong can be essential and if others can help, all the better. This is also true in school, business, or your profession.

So the reactions of sympathetic, sensitive people can be indispensable, as when you're informed that someone already wrote the article. Advisors may provide additional insight, clues to the puzzle, intensify, not weaken, your resolve. Besides, good

ideas have lives of their own, and don't easily sur-
render.

Evaluation is a virtue of writing classes which
should contribute courage if at all deserved (students permitted to tear each other's work to bits
have poor instructors), but you must be able to take
suggestions without bristling. Confident writers
can evaluate what others tell them. A strong ego
won't crumple like a rose.

It's axiomatic that lovers, mothers, and relatives
are the worst critics, in that order, because they're
biased in your favor. The acid test is to submit for
publication and learn from the responses of agents
and editors. Then, like it or not, you must heed their
opinions, including rejections.

Some successful writers like to claim they spit on
reviews, but they might profit by taking bad ones
seriously. Criticism can be desperately erratic, but if
there's a common denominator in what the critics
say the writer ought to listen at least. Listening
doesn't mean agreeing.

JARGON AND CLICHÉS

They are not the same. Jargon is the "buzzwords"
(clichés) of an "in-group" (jargon) that seeks verbal
shortcuts and to impress others with its skill or
knowledge. A cliché is a word or phrase employed
so frequently that it's dead on arrival.

Stay away from both if you can.

"Authoring" is quite as unacceptable for a writer as "vivid impression," "significant other," "lifestyle," "wannabees" etc., etc., etc. One objective of writing is freshness where possible, and if you can't change the tide of our language, littered as it is with jargon and clichés, at least you can change your habits. Use such verbiage only with derision.

HOW TO RECOGNIZE BAD WRITING

Why so many intelligent people, including and especially teachers, have such trouble turning out a decent sentence is something of a mystery. Lack of discipline may be a reason, and a certain pretentiousness is common to some.

Defensiveness may figure, too, for if a notion were presented in a clear way that could be quickly understood, whose meaning was unarguable, everyone might laugh at the obviousness of it. Or, the writer may not know what he or she is talking about. The murkier the thought, the more obtuse the language is likely to be. The more pretentious the writer, the sillier he is apt to sound.

You can often spot bad writing, including mine and yours, by the overuse of italics, dots, dashes, and parentheses, often indicating undigested or pilfered material, perhaps inserted after the basic text was done and which, at any rate, the writer has not bothered to assimilate into the body of the work.

Watch for gummy language, or too many adjectives and adverbs (the curse of popular fiction). These are words that don't have specific roles to play. (Used properly, a word, like a good chess move, can perform several functions at once. Study the interconnections.)

Please, please abandon the wise-words, such as "writerwise." Be especially watchful for the overuse of pronouns like "it." *The New York Times* could save a fortune in computerized typesetting if aware (not "were it aware") that the "it" in its incessant "made it clear" is unnecessary. "Made clear" is better language. Such hidden redundancies are increasingly common and, like too much salt, should be avoided, as with "just" and "really," when they add nothing.

"He just really couldn't," when "he couldn't" would have sufficed. As for "check it out" (why "out"?), pack it in.

Also, be wary of a faulty paragraph sense—that is, an inability to exercise logical discretion between thoughts, to know when to stop and start again. There are reasons for paragraphs as reflected by pauses in speech and speeches. The reader (listener) must be given a chance to absorb what's been said. A paragraph that is too long is a gauntlet the reader may not pick up.

LOOSE ENDS

You don't want to leave loose ends or holes that

you'll have to go back and laboriously fill. A solution may be notes, constantly reminding yourself of what remains to be done. (I'm a great believer in notes.) You're keeping, in effect, a detailed record to tell you what you're in danger of leaving out.

Aristotle's notion of bad art was "one thing after another," by which he meant a motley collection of incidents without cohesion or purpose. Your vision ought to be balanced and complete.

Now you're on the home stretch! And you thought you'd never make it!

You see the finish line ahead and what an immense satisfaction it gives you. You persevered and that achievement can't be taken away. But slow up. You're only racing yourself. Take a deep breath. How precisely do you wish to end? On what illuminating or suspenseful note? Rather, perhaps, than you finding it, inspiration might find you.

That's the final tip. Don't hurry. Wait.

NOW IS IT FINISHED?

You've reread once more and the feeling persists

that you're finished, though you never believed you would be.

You may find yourself thinking that if you had to construct it again you'd proceed differently, but that's no reason of itself to start over. Have you done your best at this stage of your development? The distinction is important: You may, and should, be improving, and while the work just completed might not be quite up to what you'll be able to do in the future, it's as good as you could manage until now. You don't want a premature birth on your hands but you don't want to be overly harsh on yourself either.

So if instinct thus informs you, it may be time to cease, because further effort may be useless and even detract. Save your strength for the next task, which you should already be planning.

SUBMITTING (IF THAT'S THE GOAL)

Which of you in the audience, secretly or not, would like to publish in whatever forum? Stand up. Almost all of you, it seems.

Strictly speaking, writing better has little to do with being published but for many that is the real goal and goad.

Composers want audiences, painters want viewers, writers want readers. To have them, you must publish, and you will require a publisher, unless you wish to take on the arduous task of typesetting, printing, warehousing, distribution, advertising, and sales on your own. (If your aim is not to be a published writer, good for you. Skip the next few paragraphs.)

If possible, find a literary agent to handle your material (but not generally for short works: The payoff for agents is too small.) Any writer who begrudges the ten or fifteen percent an agent charges has rocks in his head. Agents are invaluable: They know the market, save you the trouble of mailing and the pain of rejection, and they understand contracts and money. Publishers prefer to deal with them because they are a sort of guarantee of your professionalism—publishers may not even read agentless manuscripts. In fact, sad to say, if serious efforts do not yield an agent, your writing career, if you intend one, may be in jeopardy. Or, at best, your manuscript may require a drastic overhaul.

Consider the real situation, not the one in TV movies about writers. A sizable book house will receive 20–30,000 proposals a year, the great majority of which are discarded. Yet even after that, the winnowing process continues until the editors agree on the 300–400 books a year a large firm will publish. Yours, you intend, will be one of them.

But you simply cannot rely on luck, fate, or even your talent. Book houses are uncertain, mercurial, fearful. The editors you deal with are usually sensitive, dedicated, and smart, but, reflecting their business, they are not without insecurity. (And vanity: Check to see what the editor has written, if anything, read it, mention that you have.) They will want to be convinced your project can succeed.

Put yourself in their place. All those choices! All those mistakes that publishers make and only partly because the public's fickle. Those (probably underpaid) editors don't care to be guilty of publishing errors and demand, sometimes unreasonably, that you help them not to. They wish you to explain your notion as carefully as possible, which should make them your allies because they can prevent you from wasting time.

Before you submit, you and/or your agent ought to have a grasp of the marketplace—what various publishers specialize in, have confidence in, are good at. Book houses vary. Read their ads in *Publishers Weekly*, the bible for the book trade. Look at subject material in the library and *Books in Print*. Then, having made some decisions about publishers, if you're agentless, find an editor's name in a book for writers that lists them. To deal directly with an actual person in this, as in any other area, is urgently necessary.

Save the editor work—that will be a plus. Start with a well conceived letter. (This advice is not simply for the millions of unwashed writers but is culled from a bulletin of the Authors Guild, a professional society. Its members, too, apparently, have to be told.) Explain: Why is the book needed? Who will read it? What books on the subject have been written? Why are you qualified and why do you want to write it? You ought to convey your excitement, but in a controlled manner. Don't froth at the mouth. Don't you distrust people who oversell?

Behind your letter should be a ten page, or so, proposal with the same material, though in more detail, illuminating what you want to say and conveying the flavor. There ought to be a chapter outline as well and, for fiction, a summary of the plot. You should mention that you are prepared to present a sample chapter or two—the editor, if interested, will certainly ask for that—and, if you feel supremely confident, you can enclose the chapters without waiting.

For books, and other material too, be certain to have a page that explains your concept for how the product should be marketed.

Try to communicate the quality of your mind. Show the best and only the best. Never attach a defensive note that says, "I know this needs editing." Check your spelling and punctuation. Do not turn in material about which you have doubts. Do not squander the precious moment when your work will be scrutinized—you may have only one shot at the editor (or superior) so don't blow it. You want to display your merits, not weaknesses.

You might consider a university press if you're not an established writer, and even if you are. More than one out of six books published today bears a university press imprint, and a few, including fiction, have been bestsellers. You can't usually expect to make money but the average university press book remains in print much longer than those of commercial houses which will drop books in less than a year if they don't sell—weeks, in the case of softcover fiction.

Director L.E. Phillabaum, of the Louisiana State University Press, which published *A Confederacy of Dunces*, a novel that won the Pulitzer Prize, says, "It is important that an author become informed about specific university presses before sending them a manuscript, and be realistic about marketing activities...also the evaluation process can be an extended one," since committees have to approve. Still, if you do quality work, are willing to settle for a limited audience, desire prestige, and burn to publish, a university press might be your best bet.

Also, the small press scene is active today. It's the home of new writing (poetry and experimental prose) which rarely finds support from commercial publishing houses. Literary magazines and the small presses document new trends and provide young writers with forums. The frustrations are distribution and a tendency to publish writers from their own circles.

Small Press Distribution in Berkeley, California, is one of the distribution services set up to help the small presses find literary outlets and serious readers. Enterprising small presses have tried to move into the terrain of bigger houses, and some, like

North Point, have even had bestsellers, such as *West With the Night.*

Others, like Black Sparrow, Station Hill, The Pushcart Press, and North Atlantic, have broadened their lists and gained commercial success. For writers, the move from a small to a larger publishing house can be made. Ultimately, though, the small press is known for its dedication and noncommerciality. (For small press listings, see writers' handbooks.)

HARD CHOICES

Where you stand in the army of writers may well depend on decisions you make, little by little or all at once, on what sort of writing you'll undertake and how much risk you're able to endure.

If you're a poet, you know in advance that writing will never support you (unless you're a sentimental one like Rod McKuen, who must have made some very unsentimental decisions about his audience.) Similarly, if your work espouses left wing or "green" causes, you had better find a teaching job, or come up with a *Whole Earth Catalogue.*

Whether you can tolerate the financial and ego uncertainties of being an independent writer—writers always become discouraged sometimes and must expect difficult periods—is a question you should ponder. It's at least prudent to have some published work behind you before you notify your accountant you're about to be self-employed.

Occupation: Writer (as Robert Graves put it) is a worthy title and the IRS will let you take deductions in lean years, assuming you had income to deduct against.

Freelance commercial writers should and may select their weapons as carefully as medieval knights on a battlefield. They may deliberately choose subjects and styles in terms of what they know their audience will buy. Generally, though, if bestselling writers like Robert Ludlum and the late Louis L'Amour write the same book over and over, it's because the genre interests them, perhaps because they do it well.

The seasoned professional knows that he must be ahead of the foot soldiers but not very far: The avant garde may be cut down or ignored, which is approximately the same.

Don't suppose for a moment that "literary" writers can't calculate, too, building the critics into their thinking as the "freelance" does sales. You can be superb but still worry about your reputation and hope for a prize. To win the Nobel Prize for Literature requires *sitsfleysch* in spades.

Which is not to say that most independent writers don't merely sit down and ply their craft as energetically as possible. For them, risk comes to seem built in to the profession, since they've lived with it for so long.

The Rewards

Payoffs of various kinds: monetary, psyche,
humanitarian. The corporate vantage.
Feeding the lake.

Some write because they have to, seemingly oblivious to, and even in defiance of, personal benefits. Call them dedicated, driven, compulsive, masochistic, fanatical, as you will, yet write they must. Thomas Wolfe scribbled away on his deathbed.

Most of us aren't possessed by the writing demon. You may have to remind yourself of the tangible and intangible rewards. When you strive for achievement as a writer bear in mind, as a goal, how you may benefit. You've studied, practiced, produced, but you may still need the motivation to continue, to tolerate the difficulties, to go on writing.

The practical benefits from good writing may be extensive in academia, the professions and most other occupations. Writing well can make the difference in grades, honors, being published in learned journals. It can mean promotions, raises and prestige (if that's what you desire, or must have, to climb). It can strongly affect your life if only because you have increased your powers of discipline (the *sitsfleysch* system), concentration, organization, language. You will have a competitive advantage.

In corporations, writing well will enable you to establish visibility and identity. Though you may sometimes think so, a business doesn't want to be populated by faceless, slavish creatures even as it may not tolerate eccentricity. A corporation should, and mostly does, encourage self-expression in its tight little world. A middle-level executive may write or receive for criticism a three-inch stack of interoffice memos, letters, "status reports" (jargon), proposals, and so on in a single week. He or she is virtually guaranteed a forum if he or she knows, literarily, how to use it.

They have the chance, within limits, of course, to display ideaophoria (the ability to produce ideas), humor, integrity, profit-mindedness, but they (or you) had better communicate in a fashion that will seize the day. Otherwise, brilliant contributions will pass unnoticed and be, therefore, useless.

Psychological rewards figure, too. To have trouble expressing yourself on paper leads to frustration just as ease in doing so yields confidence. It's no accident that confidence has become a by-word; technological society can be hard on self-esteem because people become as parts of a machine. Writing well is an expression of individuality in the computer age.

Since society is so demanding, writing, if only for your own consumption, can offer a sort of sanctuary.

"You get a lot off your chest," said novelist John Dos Passos. "And to use language effectively is a satisfaction of itself."

With regard to income for those who write on their own, it smells. The majority of self-employed writers earn from the trade less than $5,000 a year. Even successful writers may make less than you think, but never before have a few writers garnered so much from best sellers, in hard and soft covers, foreign sales, and entertainment rights. The great majority, though, must be content with being gentlemen (and gentlewomen) writers who, like gentlemen farmers, are in there for pleasure.

You've decided who you write for—you, your friends, associates, a public no matter how small. Whichever, enjoyment resides in the ability, and maybe some social responsibility is involved, too. We should, or so we're taught, have obligations to our own society if not the world (though it sometimes seems neither has obligations to us) and writing is a basic part of it. So are writers. As observed by Ezra Pound in *The ABC of Reading*:

> *"Writers as such have a definite social function exactly proportional to their ability AS WRITERS. That is their main use...If a nation's literature declines, the nation atrophies and decays."*

Pound wrote that while the average American family watched TV almost endlessly, tested verbal skills fell for eighteen straight years. Between twenty and forty percent of the adult population is illiterate, (with the "lowest reading skills," according to the Department of Education's euphemism) in a nation that spends $7 billion in video games, more than for books and motion picture tickets combined.

Efficient and accurate writing is, and will be, more and more, a social necessity. It is for the writer to strip away incorrect language, protecting it from pollution and political exaggeration, to better it, and to spread the joy of words.

Perhaps you should tell yourself as well that you might have something to say. Maybe you teach in your own fashion, like J. D. Salinger, who spoke of leaving signs along the road. Maybe you believe your brand of personality is something the others should know about.

James Jones wanted to impose himself "on the world. . .want people to know how I have lived."

(**Note**: some of these quotes are from the *Paris Review* series.)

William Gass: "I write because I hate. A lot. Hard."

To novelist Irving Wallace: "I've worked in, I think, every medium. I started out writing plays and for magazines always. I had one thing in my mind, that I wanted to write books because I felt that was the last independent thing. The big terrible hangup I had—maybe it wasn't a hangup—was that I didn't want to be a boss. I didn't want to work for anyone; I didn't want to be an employee..."

For Norman Mailer: "...you're in love with the truth when you discover it at the end of a pencil. That, in and by itself, is one of the rare pleasures of life."

Hemingway talked of "a sense of justice and injustice" as a reason to write.

To William Gaddis, "Perhaps my mission as a writer is to save our country with my own vision of our country."

John Updike pointed to the writer's "grimly jaunty independence."

Said E.B. White, "I feel that a writer has an obligation to transmit, as best as he can, his love of life, his appreciation for the world. Writing is an act of faith, nothing else. And it must be the writer, above all others, who keeps it alive—choked with laughter or with pain."

Poet Jean Rhys reminded that writers are part of

a tradition: "I want to tell you something very important. All of writing is a huge lake. There are great rivers that feed the lake, like Tolstoy and Dostoevsky. And there are trickles, like Jean Rhys. All that matters is feeding the lake. It is very important. Nothing else is important."

How to Write...Faster!

Word Processors
by
Daniel B. Diner, Ph.D.

You want to be a writer, but you're afraid to use a computer. Then you've got a problem. If you want to compete in today's market, then you've got to use a word processor. Why? Because they're so good.

In fact, they're the best tool in town.

WHY NOT BUY A WORD PROCESSOR?

The three most common reasons why people who write things hesitate to buy a word processor are, in order, fear, fear, and fear.

Let's discuss them one at a time.

REASON 1: FEAR.

The first reason is fear. Fear that computers are too hard to use.

After all, they include math, don't they? Won't they make me feel stupid?

It's true, computers include math, but word processors don't call upon your math skills at all. And they won't make you feel stupid. They'll probably make you feel pretty smart once you get going.

It's similar to learning to drive a car. You don't have to be a master mechanic who understands all the intricacies of internal combustion to drive a car. And although it may take a bit of practice to be a truly great driver, the benefits of driving are realized from the start. Ask any teenager.

People interested in word processing today are very lucky. This is because the widespread use of computers in the office and the home have supported remarkably rapid growth in the computer industry. The growth is not only in technical capability, but also in the ease of use. The technical term for this is **"user friendly."**

Today's modern word processors are designed to

make their usage easy for anyone, no matter how non-technical they may be. Most features are **menu driven**, which means that the computer screen displays in everyday English a menu full of things you can do. And like eating out, all you have to do is order what you'd like. And like the joy of eating, the joy of creating is reserved for you.

There is tremendous competition in the industry right now, with heavy emphasis on making their products accessible to you. After all, you, the non-users, are the untapped market and the race is on. This is one of those rare cases where the non-technical are driving a technical market.

Take advantage of it.

Reason 2: Fear.

The second reason is fear. Fear the computer will ruin your creativity.

After all, computers are inhuman. They sit there and make noise. They are mechanical, unfeeling, an invasion to the serenity of the writer's garret. They make so many things automatic that the romance and excitement of writing will be lost.

Wrong. If you believe any of this, then you just don't know what's available. The outstanding success of word processing today is due to the fact that they *make writing easier*. As described in this chapter, a word processor can remove most of the drudgery and busy work from the craft of writing,

WORD PROCESSORS—BY DANIEL B. DINER

and leave you free to create. Consider the word processor your brand new sports car, ergonomically whisking you through paradise, as you gaze out through your own unique goggles, recording all that you find worthy.

REASON 3: FEAR.

The third reason is fear. Fear it's too expensive, not worth the price.

Here again, the person interested in word processing today is lucky. The office and entertainment markets for computers have driven the affordable technology way beyond the needs of word processing. The end result? Many very powerful word processing programs fit on computers which are already several generations old. A generation in the computer world is about a year or two. So some pretty powerful stuff is being closed out at bargain prices.

The time you save using your word processor will far outweigh its cost. And long before you finish depreciating it for your taxes.

WHY BUY A WORD PROCESSOR?

Three major problems for the writer that word processors solve immediately are organization, lost notes, and writer's block.

Organization is solved by the capability to move

sections of text about in a document. You need not begin at the beginning, as Lewis Carroll had to do. You can begin anywhere, because you can insert and move text about with the greatest of ease.

Lost notes are a thing of the past. Of course, if you insist, you can still lose notes. (Some of us love antiquity.) But if you simply discipline yourself to enter all of your ideas into your word processor the first time you write them, then you will always have them. When you find exactly the right place for one, you can instantly copy it into your current document and still keep the original version of it. I keep a file called "Tidbits" into which I place any idea as soon as it comes into my head. When I drive my car, I keep a microcassette recorder with me. As soon as I get home, I enter any new ideas into Tidbits.

Writer's block is probably the greatest enemy of all would-be writers. The terror of not being able to start a piece of work because the opening sentence just can't be found, has driven many a would-be writer to take a day job. But with the word processor, you can just start anywhere. You can always fill in the rest later. When the tiniest part of a plot reveals itself to you, just start typing.

I often start a difficult piece with the words, "Okay, so guys think I'm just a drunk in a bar. And maybe I am. But let me tell you a story about...." Later, I remove all the personal dialogue with my imagined innebriates, and I'm left with a partially completed story!

What Can a Word Processor Do for You?

Quite a lot. First of all, there is **error correction**. When you find a typo, you simply delete the erroneous letter or letters, and type in the correct ones. Finished.

Next is the **cut and paste** function. Suppose you find that a wonderful section of prose belongs in an entirely different part of your document. In a matter of seconds (literally) you can move all, or any parts of that section, to where you want. If you don't like the new location, then simply cut and paste it again. Suppose you need to repeat something more than once. Then you use the **copy and paste** function, which again only takes seconds, no matter how large a section of text you are copying.

Suppose you have several similar passages, or equations in a technical report, which may be rather complicated or tedious to type out. Just copy the first one as many times as you need, and edit each copy accordingly. Sometimes I wonder if Moses used the copy command on the Ten Commandments. That would explain why so many of them start with, Thou shalt not....

The **wrap around** function is one you'll just love. You just keep typing, and the word processor inserts the line breaks wherever they are needed. If you delete or insert any characters or words, the wrap around function will adjust all of the following text for you in that paragraph. No more having to use the poetically wrong word just because it fits in the space available. Since the invention of movable type, we writers have waited for this particular freedom.

The **insert** function is also extremely useful. Suppose after typing five perfect pages you realize that you forgot to explain that the prince looked exactly like the pauper. Horror of horrors. Time to retype the whole thing, and the report is due tomorrow. No worry, simply move the **cursor** (your place-holder in the document) to the right place, and insert all the text you need. Not only will the word processor make room for the insertion, but it will even adjust the following page breaks for you automatically (if you tell it to).

Then you realize that you forgot to call Jekyll, "Dr." Jekyll. Have no fear! Just use the **search and replace** function to change "Jek" to "Dr. Jek" throughout the document. You don't even need to write out "Jekyll" in full if you're sure you only use "Jek" in his name and nowhere else. You can even tell the word processor to show you each change before it makes it, and to only make the change if you approve it. You can also search for "Jek" throughout the document, just in case you forgot to capitalize the good doctor's name. And like everything else, this can be done, literally, in seconds, even though you might have thousands of "Jekles" to correct.

Then you realize that you might have spelled some of those technical terms incorrectly. That means a good half hour at the dictionary? Not in the 90s. Just run the **spell checker**, and all will be well. Maybe you'll want to approve the changes before they're made, just to be doubly sure. You don't want those strange European names to be changed into properly spelled English adverbs.

Now it's one A.M., and you reread the instructions the professor gave out. Or maybe the formatting requirements the literary journal sent you. Suddenly, you realize your margins are too wide! Start retyping? Maybe your parents had to, but all you do is change the **margin settings** and you're finished. For more complicated changes, such as **page formatting**, just type a couple of commands and the entire document is re-formatted.

Did you forget the page numbering? Or did you put them in when the prof said not to? No problem. One command and it's corrected. Sure beats centering and typing two hundred page numbers and remembering not to duplicate or skip a number. You can also select whether to have the first page numbered, and whether to have the numbers **centered, left justified,** or **right justified,** and placed at the top or the bottom of the page.

Did they say pica, and you used elite? No problem. Just change the font size, and once again you're finished. And while you're there, maybe you'd prefer to use **Helvetica condensed**, *Times italics*, or `Courier`.

Did you want to write something with a superscript, such as 3^2, or a subscript, such as A_3? Just tell your word processor and it's yours. What about underline or *italics* or perhaps something smaller or perhaps something larger? It's all there waiting for your command. Did you need some foreign language characters . . . é, ö, û? No problem. We've got them all, just waiting for you. No need to get out that rapidograph and your steadiest hand. Just click your mouse on the proper boxes, and everything is yours. Welcome to the 90s.

And that's not all. Did you want to see how your document looks in double space or one and a half space? That's so easy, I'm embarrassed to show you. Let's just copy the paragraph above in one and a half space, and see how it looks:

Did you want to write something with a superscript, such as 3^2, or a subscript, such as A_3? Just tell your word processor and it's yours. What about underline or *italics* or perhaps something smaller or perhaps something larger? It's all there waiting for your command. Did you need some foreign language characters . . . é, ö, û? No problem. We've got them all, just waiting for you. No need to get out that rapidograph and your steadiest hand. Just click your mouse on the proper boxes, and everything is yours. Welcome to the 90s.

Let's go back to single space, but this time flush right. Piece of cake.

Did you want to write something with a superscript, such as 3^2, or a subscript, such as A_3? Just tell your word processor and it's yours. What about underline or *italics* or perhaps something smaller or perhaps something larger? It's all there waiting for your command. Did you need some foreign language characters . . . é, ö, û? No problem. We've got them all, just waiting for you. No need to get out that rapidograph and your steadiest hand. Just click your mouse on the proper boxes, and everything is yours. Welcome to the 90s.

Again, in just seconds, you can change your whole document to the style of your choice. And you can see it ahead of time! Speaking of that, how about a **page preview** before you print?

What's a page preview? Good guestion. Most word processor screens do not show you an entire page at one time. To do so, either the screen must be quite large, or the type must be very small.

Large screens cost more (and can be purchased), whereas small type is difficult to read. Thus, the standard industry compromise of showing about half a page at a time is not bad at all.

Sometimes, however, you may want to see a whole page at once, and the function name for viewing a whole page in smaller type is page preview. A poet might find that very useful. Or, if you write a lot of business letters, you can use the page preview feature to help keep your letters down to a single page. Simply preview your page before you print it out, and edit it, or change the margins, or change the line spacing, etc. This saves you a lot of time and printer paper. Besides, people are more likely to read a one-page letter.

Alternatively, you can buy a system with a full-sized 8½ inch by 11 inch monitor.

Mail merge routines make writing letters and addressing envelopes a breeze. You can send many individualized letters out, but only type one general letter. You can even set up your mail merge so that as the system prints the letters on the mailing list, it automatically varies the context of the letter to fit the person it is being sent to. This is not limited to the name and address. It can include other features as well. For example, you might not want to send the same New Year's greeting to your married ex-lovers as to your unmarried ex-lovers.

Modern mail merge function can find the address in the letter and print the envelope automatically.

Of course, you can automatically print label lists, which should dramatically improve your winter holiday season.

There are many other functions, such as making your own standard **headers**, and **footers**. For example, every time you write a letter, your address, phone number, business logo, and even the current date can be put on top of the letter, automatically.

The features go on and on. Automatic **undo commands** (so you can undo any edits or accidents that you don't like), automatic **footnote** handling, **table of contents** and **index** generation, **single** or **multiple** column formats, creation and insertion of **tables** and **graphics** figures, automatic **grammar checking** (for those of us who make such errors). You can even get automatic **character**, **word**, **line**, **sentence**, **paragraph**, and **page counts**, which is wonderful if you are paid by the document length. And for those of us who forget to be brief, how about that **average sentence length count**!

Redlining and **strikeout** are features which merit some in-depth discussion. Suppose you would be crazy enough to co-author a book. Your partner in this crime sends you a 300-page first draft to look at. You pop his or her disk into your computer and immediately start striking out all sorts of extraneous stuff and inserting some absolute brilliance in its place. Yet, your co-author has an established reputation, something that you are trying to build for yourself. You hesitate to send back a 125-page version of the draft, but you know it's a better version. Besides, you want your mentor to see how deftly you sliced away the ugly fat from this future masterpiece! And, you want your new version and the old version to be immediately available to your mentor's word processor and printer. An additional requirement: your mentor must be able to select and reject any of your many edits easily on his or her word processor.

So give me something hard to do! All this can be easily accomplished by using the redlining and strikeout features. They will highlight the inserts (redlines), overprint the deletions (strikeouts) with dashes through the characters, identify any text that was moved, and will enable you to choose how to print the document. Your printing choices include either with the highlighting, overprinting, and text movements marked, or in final edited form with all the redline text inserted (but not highlighted) and none of the strikeout text printed at all. And best of all, your mentor can pop your disk into his or her word processor and keep or remove your edits easily.

You can print your documents either horizontally (**landscape**) or vertically (**portrait**) on the page. You can even send and receive a fax directly by your computer. No more stupid fax paper documents lying rolled up on your desk. You can even edit the faxes you receive before you print them, or cut and paste parts of them into another document.

With the right software and a good printer, you can even do **desktop publishing**. I recently co-authored a scientific book complete with graphs, tables, mathematical equations and numerous scientific drawings. Except for a couple of photographs and hand-drawn medical pictures, we desktop published the entire book. The publishers literally photographed the laser-printed pages we sent them. My co-author and I did this for our own personal convenience, and the publisher even upped our royalty percentage because they didn't have to typeset the book.

I recently bought a **software package** for under fifty dollars which enables me to make greeting cards on my computer. It will print out the paper so that with one or two folds, I have a totally custom made card for every friend and every occasion that may arise. Please understand that I can print the greetings in some pretty impressive sizes and styles. For example:

HAPPY

61st

BIRTHDAY

Arthur

Not bad, considering that it only took me seconds to write that. By the way, I did that without the greeting card software. Understand one thing here, **I got power.**

What System Should I Buy?

I thought you'd never ask!

There's a lot of neat stuff out there. And, like anything else, it depends on your needs and your budget. But don't worry, 'cause the prices are right.

As mentioned above, the office and entertainment markets for computers have driven the technology way beyond the needs of personal word processing. End result? Perfectly fantastic word processing programs can be run on computers which are already several generations (one or two years) old. That means last year's model can be bought at close-out prices.

So what do I recommend you get? Simple enough. Get a **laptop**. Then get either a **laser printer** or a **bubble jet printer** with a **page feeder**. The page feeder is important, because when you want to print out a long document, you don't want to sit there and feed in each page by hand. The only other thing you need is some **word processing software**.

Depending on your anticipated word-processing needs and your budget, you can choose the computer and the word processing software that best suits you. It would be inappropriate for me to suggest particular products. But I shall explain the meanings of some of the technical terms you wlll hear.

MEGABYTE, MEGAHERTZ AND RAM

Megabyte, Megahertz and **RAM** are the words you most need to understand when purchasing a computer.

MEGABYTE. What is a **megabyte**, you ask? Good question.

If I answer that a **megabyte** is not exactly a million **bytes**, you might not be happy. So that's what I'll do, but then I'll add on that a **kilobyte** is not exactly a thousand bytes, but that a byte is exactly 8 **bits**. Is that better? No? Then prepare yourself for the long answer.

One of the great challenges faced by the designers and inventors of computers was and still is to bridge the gap between human thought and electronic circuits. This means find a form of information processing that is achievable by machines and also useful to humans.

Electric currents have two basic states, off and on. So do electric switches. Therefore, the development of a code based on the off and on states is very desirable. One switch which is either off or on (or one wire which either has *no current* or has *a current*) can be assigned a code value of either 0 or 1 respectively. Now we are ready to build a computer based upon this code.

Just as a decimal digit has 10 values (0 to 9), a binary digit has only 2 values (0 to 1). A binary digit is called a **bit**. And anything we can do with decimal numbers, we can also do with binary numbers. For example, a number with three decimal digits has 10 x 10 x 10 = 1000 possible values (0 to 999) and a number with three binary digits has 2 x 2 x 2 = 8 possible values. Let's look at this closely.

With two switches, one can store 4 values. Those are 00 (both switches off), 01 (right switch only on), 10 (left switch only on), or 11 (both switches on). Read these values as 'zero zero,' 'zero one,' 'one zero', and 'one one.' With 3 switches, one has 8 possible values: the four above with the third switch off, and the four above with the third switch on.

Of course, this can be extended. Four switches gives 16 values and 8 signals gives 256 possible values.

Now in wiring up series of switches, it is always easy to do things in powers of 2 (2, 4, 8, 16, 32, ...). Just add another layer of switches, also 8 switches is a nice unit electronically. But is it useful for information coding and information processing? If it is, then it is a natural building block for the bridge between electronic circuits and human information processing.

Well, what could be interesting about a 256-value code?

Plenty. With 256 values, one can easily define a code in which every letter (caps and lower case), all the digits, punctuation marks, many mathematical symbols, foreign letters such as ç and even symbols like ✿ and ☐ are represented. True, 7 bits could have coded all the letters and many symbols. But 7 is less desirable electronically than 8. And besides, 8 gives double the number of characters.

So 8-bit units won the honor of becoming the basic building block of computer information processing and (because all the letters and punctuation symbols are represented) word processing. And it was given a name, and the name was **byte**.

Each time you type a character into your computer, it takes one byte to store it. One byte of what? Great question. One byte of computer memory. What is computer memory? Another great question. It really is a pleasure to write a chapter for you.

Computer memory is magnetic memory. Basically it works as follows. A magnetizable material (like a tape cassette) is magnetized (by passing a current through it) to point either upward or downward. Then, the direction of that magnetization can be sensed whenever needed, provided it does not lose its orientation. Again, this acts like a binary digit—a bit. If it points downward (say) it represents 0. If it points upward it represents a 1. Put 8 of them together in their own private circuit and they become one byte of magnetic memory.

Humans like decimal numbers. We even have

special names for the ones we love the most, such as "hundred," "thousand," and "million." Electronic circuit builders like powers of 2, such as 256, 512, 1024.... Hey, look out! That's a pretty attractive little power of two you've got there, 1024. She reminds me a lot of an old favorite of mine, 1000. How about this? You build me a unit of 1024 bytes, and I'll learn to love her the way I love 1000. I'll even give her a nickname. Will "kilobyte" be okay?

And that's why a kilobyte is not exactly 1000 bytes. And, yep, you guessed it, a megabyte is 1024 kilobytes.

Now for the only quiz question in this section. Roughly, how many single-spaced typed pages of text could you store in 20 megabytes of computer memory?

Bet you never thought you'd be able to answer a question like that fifteen minutes ago. See why I love writing for you? You're a natural in this field! So, let's get the answer.

Depending on your type size, you can figure between 80 and 120 characters per line and 66 lines per page. To play safe, let's say 8000 characters per page. Divide 8000 into 20 million and you get 2,500. So 20 megabytes will hold roughly 2,500 single-spaced, jam-packed, typed pages. Damn, you're good!

What? You think I made a mistake? No. I just didn't get to it yet. Or maybe this is the second time you're reading this chapter. Do you want to explain what you just said to the other readers? Go ahead. You certainly don't need to be shy when you're home alone reading a book.

Well, maybe you're right. Maybe they won't be able to hear you. Okay, I'll explain it, and I'll repeat what you say. Okay, readers, this is not me speaking anymore, but that very clever reader over there who wants you all to know that you get almost a million extra bytes which means about 125 extra single-spaced pages.

"What I want to say is that a megabyte is actually 1024 x 1024, or 1,048,578 bytes. So 20 megabytes is almost 21 million bytes. That's all."

Well done. First time I ever had a future reader tell me what to write. But you did an excellent job of it. Thank you.

So let's see if I can get this chapter back under control. By the way, can you imagine how difficult all this would be without a 20 megahertz computer chip on my side? Megahertz? What's a megahertz? Good question. But first let me finish this 2,500 page thing. Yes, I mean 2,625 pages.

Computer systems have a variety of memory back-up systems. So 2,500 is the number of pages that you can work with *simultaneously* with 20 megabytes of free memory. Of course, some of your computer memory will be used to store other things such as your word processor program, the computer's operating system, and any other software you might want. So you must pay attention to how much memory is left over after all your software is installed. Even so, don't be too worried. Twenty megabytes is not a lot of memory at all nowadays.

MEGAHERTZ. Now let's talk about megahertz. A **megahertz** is 1024 kilohertz. A **kilohertz** is 1024 **hertz**. Hertz is a measure of frequency and it literally means "cycles per second." It is used when discussing the **computer processor speed.** (The computer processor is the chip that does the information processing. It is not the software that does the word processing.) It is actually a measure of how fast the computer clock ticks. The less complex computer commands take only a few clock ticks. More complicated commands may take many clock ticks. Reading the keyboard, echoing the keyboard input to the screen, and storing the characters in memory only take a few clock ticks per character typed. And this is all the computer has to do while you are typing your great American novel. So unless you type faster than Superman on steroids, your typing should never be slowed by a 20 megahertz system. By the way, a 20 megahertz system is a slow system these days.

RAM. The first three letters of a three letter word with many meanings. But what does it mean when someone says, "This machine has four megabytes of RAM?"

RAM stands for Random Access Memory. This is memory that you can write on and read from. It is also memory that is hooked up directly to the processor chip and therefore can be read very quickly. In contrast, hard disk memory is not hooked up directly to the processor chip, and is much slower to read. The difference can be very noticeable.

For example, every now and then, you may hear a spinning sound and notice a lag between your typing some text and the appearance of that text on the screen. At that point, your computer is probably accessing the hard disk. Don't worry, though. Even Superman must wait for a slow disk drive. But no one waits for RAM, simply because it's directly wired in. Therefore, RAM is good stuff to have enough of.

Depending on the word processor you intend to use, you may need very different amounts of RAM. Rather than give you numbers that might be meaningful as I write this but are quite quaint by the time you read this, I'll simply say that you should know what software you intend to use, and get enough RAM to do the job elegantly. By the way, most computers allow you to purchase extra RAM and simply plug it in. Be sure you pay attention to RAM. It is important.

What Software Should I Buy?

The answer is quite simply, "Buy what you need, today. By the time you need more, the prices will have dropped." So how do you determine what you need today?

The first thing you must decide is with whom you must be **compatible**. If you must hand a computer disk to them which they can pop into their machine and immediately read your work, and vice versa, then you must find out how fussy their hardware and software are. Most modern word processing systems can read the output of most other word processing systems. Some, however, may be more fussy than others. This is particularly true if your compatibility partner is using older software. In that case, you might be able to convince your partner to upgrade to a more modern word processor.

The next question is what type of system will you be most comfortable using. Do you like using a **mouse** or **trackball**, or are you an ex-computer jock and you want to use control keys (special function keys) and typed commands? It's something like marriage. Compatibility and happiness need not be mutually exclusive.

Tips for Computer Shoppers

Now you have enough information to go shopping. Bring along a knowledgeable friend, particularly someone with word processing experience. Spend at least a few days shopping in several different computer stores, with plenty of different computer systems set up for you to try out. Also, find salespeople who seem knowledgeable and patient. Explain it's your first system, and what you intend to use it for. Don't be shy.

If the salespeople don't seem knowledgeable, ask for their technical wizard. You may even want to phone a private computer consultant. But whatever you do, buy smart!

Consider costs as a factor. But remember that you will be using this system for many years, and a few hundred bucks today will mean nothing compared to the luxury of having a system that you feel at one with. Particularly if you intend to use your system a lot. I put my computer in the same category as my car or stereo. I don't need the very best, but I don't want second best either.

You can also save a few hundred dollars if you buy a monochrome system instead of a color system. For word processing, many writers find color more of a bother than a luxury. However, if you use extensive graphics, color is probably a necessity.

Go to a good bookstore and ask what they would recommend you read to select a computer and word processor. There are even books out, the size of a telephone book, listing hundreds of computer mail-order houses, their models and prices, and usually 800 numbers you can phone for information or to place an order. These books will, at the least, help you figure out what you should spend for equipment.

The computer journals are also well worth spending a few hours reading through. They may tell you what models break down a lot, or what software to avoid because the **bugs** (computer errors are called bugs) haven't been worked out. It doesn't hurt to call the magazine and ask someone technical what they would recommend. Computer people have a reputation for being friendly and helpful.

Another consideration is the service and user support the company provides. A 24-hour consumer help line with an 800 number can be a very important feature, especially for the beginner. Try the line before you buy. See if it is always busy, and if not, are the people helpful and friendly? Tell them your situation and see if they suggest the most expensive, up-to-date model with all the bells and whistles, or if they give you similar advice to this chapter. If they agree with me, then I trust them!

The **external memory back-up** device is something you should also inquire about. If the old standard is dying out, you may not want to start out on a doomed path. If you have used computers before, and have your old work on the old standard, you may want a system with both the old and the new standards. Or, you may find it smarter to convert your important material to the new standard now, and move forward from there.

Is the system noisy? I had a system once with a loud fan on the hard disk. The noise made me feel as if the system were constantly telling me to hurry up and write. I found this very distracting, and sold the system without having used it very much at all. And it was quite a classy system in its day.

If you are at school, find out what systems your school can offer you at an educational discount price. Quite often this discount will be 40-50% cheaper than anywhere else. You can use that to save money, or to buy a better system.

WARNINGS!

As wonderful as word processors are, one must be careful. There are pitfalls to be avoided. They deal mostly with the greatest tragedy a writer can face—the loss of his or her creative work.

If you've ever seen the face of a writer who has just lost the only copy of a manuscript that has taken several years to write, then you will read this section carefully. I have, and the only thing I said that he heard was, "Well, you can probably rewrite it in a few months from memory." He did. And he learned his lesson. I dedicate the rest of this chapter to him.

Computers are machines. They are made by humans. Both are known to fail to perform as expected on occasion.

If your computer fails catastrophically, you may lose all the information in it. One common way for this to occur is to have a **hard disk crash.** You therefore must always have back-up copies of your work on some external medium. External disks and magnetic tapes are the most common back-up devices.

I always tell my students to **keep three copies of their work on separate floppy disks.** If the system fails while you are copying your work from your hard disk to your floppy disk, you may lose both of those copies. If you have two other copies on separate floppy disks, then you can restart your computer and safely place one of the two remaining copies into the disk drive. If the system is now okay, you are on your way. If the system fails again, you still have a copy of your work on the third floppy disk, which has not been in the computer at all this session. If you only keep two back-up copies, you could not safely try to recover after the first failure.

Even three back-up disks are useless if you have not backed up any recent versions of your work. As a good rule of thumb, **back up your work to floppy disk every time you improve it**.

Learn how to care for your computer and your floppy disks. They have heat tolerance ranges. Leave your disks in the car on a very hot or very cold day, and you may lose all of your work. Check the temperature range when you buy the disks, and pay attention. The same goes for the temperature range on your computer as well.

My final warning is one that surprisingly few people know, and many do not want to believe. **Do not smoke while working on your computer.** This is not a political statement. It is for your own protection. You see, cigarette smoke molecules can get on your disk. If a smoke molecule lands on the wrong place on your disk, there is no telling how your computer may interpret the command it reads. Maybe it will think that you told it to erase everything in your computer memory. Maybe it reads it as an impossible command that it will spend hours trying to obey.

Usually when I explain this to people, they don't believe me. I've heard things like, "This computer doesn't like me. I'll be working on it and it will just stop. Then I reload the system from the back-up disk and everything's fine. It doesn't do this to other people, just me."

As they are telling me this, their cigarette is burning in the ashtray just inches away from the floppy disk drive.

What? What was that? Oh, sure. I'll tell that to the other readers for you.

Well folks, we have one final compelling reason why you should buy a laptop computer. You can write anywhere you want, even on the beach!

Further Thoughts on Word Processors

By Arthur Herzog

Some, old-fashionedly perhaps, dislike word processors: The keyboard can be difficult to master and requires sure fingers; the constant monitoring may be an irritant; between yourself and the written word, the computer intervenes with a system of its own; you may find that you can't do a first draft on one, so why bother at all? That WPs are called "processors"—are words vegetables?—may indicate a function better suited to interactive use, as on a newspaper, than to independent writing. There is factual evidence that prolonged exposure to a video screen can cause eye strain.

But this is a negative, probably minority, view. Here is the positive one.

Now, WP adepts say, no serious writer will want to use anything else. Even lazy letter writers can profit because they can write one letter to five friends by simply changing the salutation and printing it five times.

Depending on the kind of writing you do, a word processor may help you do it in a fraction of the time, and the ease of editing can improve your style and organization.

What you type appears on the screen. You can mark a word, sentence, paragraph, any block of words, and delete it or move it to anyplace in the text. That means no retyping. Instead of ruminating painfully about how you will begin, you type whatever comes to mind—even if it's the third or fourth paragraph or the middle of the story. You may then effortlessly move the cursor to the top to type in the lead, whenever that hits you. Journalists use this technique.

Organizing a long piece from notes may no longer be a nightmare. You can type everything in the order of your jottings, then move the paragraphs around till they appear in the order you want. Put in the transitions; the story is virtually done!

No more frantic typing up of final drafts. Letter quality printers run from twelve to fifty-five characters per second. That means a double-spaced page every minute or two. You can hit the print key, then go out to lunch, and pick up the finished manuscript when you come home.

Say you want to send a query to a dozen editors. You can write the letter once and, using an **auto-letter** or **mail merge** program, order it printed in sequence using the name and address of each of the names on your list.

How to buy a computer: Don't be intimidated. There are a lot of people making a lot of money teaching people about computers. Even so, unless you're learning a programming language—not necessary for most people—you can find out everything you need to know by going to free demonstrations at computer stores. Ask them to show you the word processing program on a machine that interests you. Ask to see how the program performs the basic word processing functions. Then go to another demonstration and compare.

Data Bases

Computers are not only for writing your story; they're also for researching it, and that is likely to cut the drudgery of research in the same way it ends the drudgery of writing.

You have to subscribe to a data bank like Source, Dialogue, or Nexus. There are books that list them. Instead of going to the library and spending tedious hours looking through bibliographies, indexes, or squinting at newspaper microfilm, you will type out the key words of your search (i.e., debt crisis/Argentina, 1987) and come out in minutes with bibliographic references, abstracts, or full text citations selected from thousands of publications. The data base revolution is only in its infancy.

And Finally...

Imay have erred a little on the side of strictness to be on the safe side because distraction, for the writer as for anyone else, is all too easy in a society that makes mindless entertainment almost a virtue. I tried to keep you on a narrow gauge but didn't mean to suggest you should become a robot— though someday robots may well be writers, but not the only ones, we hope.

What I may have overemphasized was WORK.

"I think," remarked Bertrand Russell, "that there is far too much work done in the world, that immense harm is caused by the belief that work is virtuous, and that what needs to be preached in modern industrial countries is quite different from what always has been preached."

Russell praised idleness, even laziness, because, he said, "Without a considerable amount of leisure a man (and woman) is cut off from many of the best things." The famous philosopher suggested that working hours be reduced to four. The result, he believed, would be that ordinary men and women would become kinder, less suspicious, and more original.

Everything should not be work. If you can't sit around a Paris café, find a substitute perhaps, even a TV set. Let yourself be inactive sometimes, ruminate, fantasize, dream...You will likely discover inner riches which your writing may soon reflect.

Nor did I intend to suggest that following similar routines will cause writers to be identical. Your spirit is your own—do the best you can with your particular, even peculiar, talent.

If you were born with a gift, as you undoubtedly were, make the most of it and be grateful.